The Power of Learning

Klas Mellander is the author or co-author of the following products and publications:

"Disco" (Teaching machine), with Hans Hofvenberg. 1962
"Basic Course in Production Methods" (Course package). 1967
"Material and Production Control" (Course package). 1968
"The Psychology of Supervision" (Course package). 1968
"Technology for High School Students" (Course package). 1968
"Financial Control" (Course package). 1969
Job Studies in Production (Book). 1970
"Applied Rationalization" (Course package). 1970
"Production Planning" (Book). 1971
A Manual for Instructors (Book). 1971
"Get it Together!" (Course package for production supervisors). 1974
"The ABCs of Company Finance" (Course package). 1976
"Get Your Office Together!" (Course package for administrative personnel). 1977
"Detail Planning" (Simulation model and course). 1977
"Industrial Production" (Course package), with Eric Giertz. 1978
"Decision Base" (Simulation model and course). 1979
"Will Choice Reality" (Training program), for Lars Wiberg. 1979
"Use Your Head" (Training program), for Tony Buzan. 1982
The Construction Process. (Book), with L. Sundsvik and J. Höjer. 1983
Project Control—A Manual for Building Contractor. (Book), with Leif Sundsvik et al. 1983
"Homo Sapiens" (Film), with M. Pieschewski and K. Nathanaelson, for SAS. 1985
"Basic Course in Production Finance" (Course package), with Eric Giertz. 1986
"Management in Times of Change" (Course package). 1988
"Sesame—The Art of Learning" (Course package). 1989
"What I Learned from not Learning" (Film). 1989
"Marketplace Livon" (Simulation model and course). 1990
"Business Decisions" with C. Ekman and M. Owens. 1991
Business Precision (Booklet). 1991
"R.O.C.E." (Simulation model and course on the productivity of capital). 1991
"Apples & Oranges" (General course in business finance). 1991

The Power of Learning

Fostering Employee Growth

Klas Mellander

 ASTD

THE AMERICAN SOCIETY FOR TRAINING AND DEVELOPMENT

IRWIN

Professional Publishing
Burr Ridge, Illinois
New York, New York

Sponsoring editor: Cynthia Zigmund
Project editor: Jane Lightell
Production manager: Ann Cassady
Compositor: Monotype Composition Company
Typeface: 11/13 New Century Schoolbook
Printer: Book Press
Designer: Lennart Frantzén
Translator: Raymond Hartman
Illustrators and Photographers: Lennart Frantzén; Jerker Eriksson; Ulf Hedetoft; Jüri Kann, Penhouse; Åke Nilsson, Illustratören AB; Lars Cardell; Ronnie Nilsson; Lasse Davidsson; IBL Bildbyrå AB; Bildarkivet Ellbergs Bilder AB

Library of Congress Cataloging-in-Publication Data

Mellander, Klas.
  The power of learning: fostering employee growth / Klas Mellander.
    p. cm.
  ISBN 1–55623–893–2
  1. Employee—Training of. 2. Employee motivation. 3. Industry and education. I. Title.
  HF5549.5.T7M435 1993
  658.3'124—dc20   92—47432

Printed in the United States of America
4 5 6 7 8 9 0 HD 0 9 8 7 6 5 4

To Linnéa

Forewords

The Power of Learning

by Warren Bennis

Warren Bennis is Chairman of the Leadership Institute, University of Southern California, and author of An Invented Life: Reflections on Leadership and Change *and* On Becoming a Leader *(Addison-Wesley, 1989 and 1993).*

In these times of boiling global change and transformation, the competitive strength of organizations has been increasingly affected by its institutional ability to learn. To learn more, better, and faster at the highest speed has become today a key strategic issue—an institutional imperative—for any organization anywhere in the world. Organizations must transform themselves into "Learning Organizations."

The purpose of teaching is to make learning possible. The picture is taken from A Manual for Instructors, *Grahm-Mellander, 1971. Since then the learner has grown up.*

This emerging concept of learning organizations must be supported by two fundamental factors. First is the key role of "Educational Leaders" in place of command and control leaders: We must go from "macho" to "maestro," from autocrats to coaches. Second is the new meaning of "self-adjusting participation" which can be defined by a clear sense of purpose and a refined competence in collective learning: an ability to be mastered by all members of the organization.

In fact, exceptional leaders have given significant attention to learning and development. Intuitively, they always tried to generate maximum group learning from the day-to-day activities and relationships of organizational life.

However, very few leaders have invested significant resources and energy—relative to what they spend on technical disciplines. Most organizations emphasize "maintenance learning," the acquisition of fixed outlooks, methods, and rules for dealing with known and recurring situations. This is necessary but not sufficient. In maintenance learning, current performance is compared only with past performance, not with what might have been or what is yet to be. The "learning organization" must rely on new competencies: acknowledging and sharing uncertainty, embracing error, responding to the future, becoming interpersonally competent (listening, nurturing, coping with value conflicts, and gaining self-knowledge). Innovative, not maintenance learning is what's needed today.

We have to ask: To what extent do today's leaders rely on innovative learning, the mastery of the art of generating deep individual and collective learning?

That's the basic question this book addresses—and it is a profound issue which our brilliant Swedish author illuminates. I should add that he has devoted the better part of his life to the art and discipline of LEARNING TO LEARN.

His timing couldn't be better! Mellander writes in a light and witty style, clear to the practitioner and, at the same time, advances the understanding to the scholar. His book is full of striking examples not only from the world of business organizations but also from the arts, literature, and other fields of human endeavor. He is a man after my own heart.

I believe that Mellander's book will contribute to helping leaders "grow" leaders at all levels of the organization. And what is more important nowadays than to help all of us understand in our hearts and in our behavior how to lead, change, and create the social architecture of a learning organization? This book is a gem in helping all of us walk, rather than back, into the future.

In a World of Change

By Bo Ekman

As head of Group Development at Volvo, Bo Ekman has had a close-up view of the roller-coaster trajectory of industry for many years. Today he leads the Swedish Institute for Opinion Research, front-line organization helping companies the world over to implement programs of strategic renewal and increases and expertise.

The average Japanese worker turns in between 30 and 40 suggestions per year on ways of increasing efficiency and improving quality. The corresponding figure at an assembly plant in Detroit, the Motor City, is one suggestion every seven years!

After an intensive campaign, Volvo doubled the number of suggestions it received to one per worker per year.

These figures dramatically illustrate a difference in both the capacity and speed with which people learn. The Japanese are able to introduce new technologies and reorganize production processes faster than the Americans and Europeans.

Over the years, companies and institutions in the Western World have been organized to function in a stable rather than changing business environment. The drawbacks of this type of organization are now becoming increasingly apparent.

We are in the midst of a painful process of reevaluating old ideas. We must question the logic behind our traditional structures and come up with new ones that enable us to cope with the turbulence caused by market fluctuations, technological advances, and the changing social conditions that are a result of people's desire to learn new ways of doing things, to change attitudes and even values, to work with new people, to interact with and learn from customers.

In this world of change, only people and organizations that have learned to learn effectively will survive. *The Power of Learning* focuses on this need and makes sound educational principles accessible to people who are seriously involved with processes of change.

This book demonstrates a deep understanding of how education can result in better leadership, and of how it can make the work of implementing change much more effective.

Preface

This book has been written both for people who want to improve their ability to learn in order to enrich their own lives, and for those who want to become more skillful in creating conditions in which others can learn—for managers, training specialists, lecturers, writers of articles and memos, instructors, project leaders, authors of manuals, video film makers, etc.

The idea behind this book took shape over twenty years ago. Åke Grahm and I had just published *A Manual for Instructors*, and we felt that nothing would be more logical as a "sequel" to that book than a manual for learning. But a couple of decades would go by before the book finally saw the light of day.

The nineties are being called the "decade of the individual." There's a new kind of respect for the individual, and a budding insight that people, not institutions, are society's driving force. Respect breeds self-respect: people today want to "get involved, really involved."

At the same time, the information explosion and the accelerating pace of change threaten to thwart even the most ambitious of us. To quote John Naisbitt, "We are drowning in information but thirst for knowledge."

If we want to avoid falling victim to other people's knowledge, we have to try to master our own.

All of this has caused people in companies everywhere to start asking themselves whether they're doing everything they can to help their employees to grow. Typical questions are: "Are they getting the overview they need to enable them to take appropriate action?" "Do they have the information they need to understand and keep track of all the twists and turns resulting from changing conditions?" "Are we taking advantage of and developing their expertise?"

A new view of the importance of learning is emerging: "The collective ability of an organization to learn is decisive for its survival," says Peter Senge in a recent book. Michael Macoby describes the new fundamental view in this way: "All people need meaning in their lives, and they're prepared to sacrifice a great deal for an organization that can give their lives meaning." Here are some of the ideas being stressed at an increasing number of companies today:

- People want (and are expected to take) greater responsibility for their own development and for the success of their organization. This motivates them to learn.
- Managers at all levels have the prime responsibility for continual expertise development (their own and their subordinates'), so they must know what's expected of them.
- Training specialists should spend less time drawing up fixed training programs for established job duties and concentrate more on strategies designed to develop expertise for specific individuals and situations.

This means that more and more people are going to have to gain an understanding of what learning really means. They must become skilled in creating conditions that promote learning in real-life situations.

I hope this book will help point the way.

Klas Mellander
Kärrshåla, Sweden

Acknowledgments

My thanks to my big sister Eva, who taught me early the importance of imagination and curiosity.

My thanks to Hans Hofvenberg (university professor), my first real teacher, who inspired me to choose the teaching profession when I was a mere 18 years old.

My thanks to Åke Grahm (M.A.), who has been my mentor all these years.

Thanks to Eric Giertz (D.Eng.), who helped me early-on to see what the conditions are in a business situation, and to understand how prevailing concepts of company development and change influence professional roles and knowledge needs.

Thanks to Krister Nathanaelson (film and TV director) who, with his feeling for the art of narration, has taught me so much about different media and the principles of drama.

Thanks to Michael Pieschewski, who helped me so often to understand my own ideas.

Thanks to Ulf and Cecilia for all their support.

Thanks to my best friend Margareta Barchan, who wisely, critically and constantly inspires me to live the way I teach.

And thanks to our little daughter Linnéa, whose debut into this exciting world prompted me to write this book.

And finally, my thanks to everyone whose unstinting efforts have helped to make this book a reality: Ella Lindsjö, Lennart Frantzén and Ray Hartman.

Contents

The Power of
Learning

1.

Learning

A lack of insight into what happens when we learn can cause us to behave quite strangely when we suddenly find ourselves in a situation in which we are taught, or study, or have to teach others.

Unlocking the mysteries of learning

Actually, learning is only difficult in connection with teaching and studying! Otherwise, people seem to learn without much effort. How else could we have assimilated the enormous amount of knowledge that we possess?

One day when I was out on a crowded street, I spotted a lady in her seventies. Leaning on her cane, she stood there, waiting for a bus. The lines in her face could have been etched by a master; they showed traces of disappointment and sadness, joy, a zest for life, and the passage of time. She stared straight ahead, not really looking at anything, apparently totally uninterested in her immediate surroundings, and with an aura of peace and tranquility enveloping her hunched-over body. Suddenly I saw her as an old, rare book with worn leather covers encasing unfathomable quantities of knowledge and wisdom. This idea must have come from the thought that every human being is a storehouse for an incomprehensible amount of information. What couldn't she tell us about all the people she's met and would recognize if she saw them again? About her experiences, emotions, friendships, times of loneliness, and the many important and unimportant events in her life? About everything she's read, heard, seen, understood, discussed, imagined and thought about? And all of this is the result of what we somewhat coldly refer to as learning—lifelong learning.

We can ask ourselves how much of her knowledge (however we care to measure it) is a direct result of formal education, and how much is simply the consequence of spontaneous, unconscious learning day after day. Even if she were a professor of nuclear physics, the answer would still be that an extremely small part of her total knowledge is a direct result of formal education and study. The same holds true for all of us.

In itself, the fact that such an incredibly small part of all learning is the result of formal education isn't especially surprising. What is much more surprising is the enormous amount of learning that takes place spontaneously, without our really being aware of it, and without any special effort on our part.

Apparently, we learn things all the time—spontaneously, and without making an effort—that seems to be practically impossible to learn in a classroom setting or with a textbook. Does this mean that we learn easier without a teacher than we do when we're taught? Oddly enough, that seems to be the case. Why?

Our ignorance induces us to complicate things for ourselves. In doing so, we diminish rather than enhance our ability to learn in a formal setting. If we can become more aware of how we learn spontaneously, we can improve our ability to learn consciously and according to plan in a formal learning situation.

You're probably attended meetings, courses, conferences, and seminars where you've sat staring fixedly at an overhead picture or a blackboard with your thoughts a thousand miles away. You've probably done the same thing while sitting with a textbook, or a manual on a company's latest product. Unable to get interested in the topic being discussed, you let your mind wander. A lack of insight into what happens when we learn can cause us to behave quite strangely when we suddenly find ourselves in a situation in which we are taught, or studying or have to teach others. Many years ago, when I was training instructors in industry, I asked them to prepare a lesson on how to set a mouse trap. When they were finished, we invited in the staff from the hotel where we were staying and asked them to act as students. The results were interesting, to say the least. The members of the hotel staff were totally lost, which isn't surprising given the instructions they received. Here are some examples: "Welcome to this lesson on how to set a mouse trap. At the conclusion of this lesson you will be capable of setting a mouse trap in accordance with the method described bla bla bla. . . ." "A mouse trap consists of the following parts: the bottom plate, a spring, a hinge, bla bla bla. . . ." "To set the mouse trap, hold it like this, between your thumb and index finger, bla bla bla. . . ." After a while, I decided to interrupt this absurd "lesson" and ask the instructors what they thought they were doing. "Why, we're teaching," they replied. I asked them whether this is what they would do if they wanted to show one of their children how to set a mouse trap. "Of course not," they replied, "but that's different. Here we're supposed to be teaching." We talked about this a great deal and noted that the way we teach changes entirely when we move to a formal classroom setting. One of the participants summed it up like this: "It's much easier to observe sound educational principles if you don't have to teach."

And that's probably true. Often, people who have learned to operate a Macintosh computer by trial and error are totally incapable of teaching others to do the same thing. The instruction they attempt to provide has absolutely nothing to do with the learning process that they themselves went through. They've already forgotten the process of experimentation and discovery they experienced, and their instruction is artificial, with loads of unnecessary facts and few, if any, opportunities for the learners to make their own discoveries. What is remarkable is that if one of these same people is asked to help someone with a computer-related problem (and thus the situation is not labeled "teaching"), his or her behavior will normally be completely different, and much more appropriate to the learner's needs.

The ways in which learners are treated in a formal training situation and in a spontaneous situation are totally different. Was this how the learners felt when they were subjected to formal instruction? (From a drawing by Lars Åberg.)

We can see a similar difference if we watch someone read. Whether it's a newspaper, a trade journal, or a book on a favorite subject, the behavior is the same: the reader leafs through the pages, stops for things that are interesting, skips over some things, reads some things in detail, backs up, compares, and so forth. But if the publication is a textbook, the behavior is different: the reader opens the book to the first page, places his or her eyes on the first word at the upper left-hand corner of the page, and starts to read, line by line by line by line. After a while, the reader's mind starts to wander, even though the eyes continue to read. And when the ambitious reader discovers this, he or she searches back to the place where assimilation ceased and tries again.

What all of this indicates is that a person in a formal situation cannot exhibit the behavior he or she would normally exhibit in a spontaneous situation. I'm convinced that the only reason for this is that most people haven't learned to observe, and thus to understand how they and other people learn spontaneously. The experience is there, but not the knowledge of how to use it.

The result is a devastating lack of effectiveness in both classroom instruction and independent study. We can even say that teaching tends to cause more pedagogical problems than it solves.

There is plenty of room for improvement, and introducing improvements isn't especially difficult. What we have to do is stop focusing our attention solely on teaching methods (as we have so far) and start concentrating on learning methods, which, as I intend to demonstrate, is something completely different. Before we get into this in detail, let me define some terms.

Teaching: the creation of suitable (external) conditions for learning, using different forms of information, exercises, assignments, etc.

Learning: the mental process that leads to knowledge.

The anecdote on the page 6 about Tiger's little brother teaching his dog to whistle is a cute way of saying that teaching doesn't always result in learning.

According to a deeply rooted idea, teachers are responsible for teaching and learners are responsible for learning, to the extent that conditions permit. This assignment of roles, or dis-

Teaching doesn't always result in learning.

tribution of responsibility, has led to an extremely sad situation: learners have gotten used to the idea that their ability to influence their instruction is close to nil. They subject themselves to their instruction rather than participate in it.

Now, the situation is beginning to change. Teachers and students are starting to share responsibility for the instruction being offered. They're helping each other to "create suitable conditions for learning." The driving force behind this new trend is that increasingly, the modern adult students want to use their time in a way that is more meaningful than merely "sitting through lessons." They look for short cuts. For the same reason, the demand for knowledge of how people learn is increasing.

This same change is taking place at the university level, and industry (a major employer of new graduates) is largely responsible. Another driving force behind this change are the students themselves, who today seem to have a much wider perspective (thanks to the media, travel, different kinds of job experience) than students 10 years ago. On the other hand, it appears that students are arriving at college with less basic knowledge from elementary and high school. This is another reason for reassessing current forms of instruction. From this point on, I'll be using the word "instructor" most of the time as a collective term for the person acting as leader in an educational setting, regardless of whether the instruction involved is a lecture, classroom instruction, a demonstration, or a presentation of information. In the same way, the term "learner" will be used to designate course participants, students, or readers of books.

I've already talked about spontaneous learning as opposed to formal learning, and spontaneous teaching as opposed to formal teaching. "Spontaneous" means that our behavior is controlled by impulses we are barely aware of, while "formal" refers to a setting that's especially designed to be "educational." We can even introduce the terms "spontaneous education" and "formal education."

My premise is that spontaneous education is consistently much more efficient than formal education, and that formal education, therefore, has a lot to learn from spontaneous education.

Physicist and Nobel Prize winner Richard Feynman has written some memoir-type books in which he often returns to the problem of teaching and learning. A couple of pertinent quotes from two of them will serve to summarize our goals and what we intend to discuss.

The first quote is from *Surely, You're Joking Mr. Feynman!*, a frank but highly constructive criticism of formal education as it is practiced in Brazil's universities. (The reader can decide how well the description coincides with his or her own experiences.) At a graduation ceremony attended by students, faculty members, and city officials, Feynman was asked to talk about his experiences during his year at the university. He asked his hosts beforehand whether he could say anything he wanted. "Sure. Of course. It's a free country," they replied. He was holding a textbook. (His hosts assumed that he intended to present it as a good example of a textbook, aware of the fact that the author was present in the auditorium.) But Feynman's opening statement showed that he had something else in mind: "The main purpose of my talk is to demonstrate that no science is taught in Brazil." A while later he held up the textbook:

> Then I held up the elementary physics textbook they were using. There are no experimental results mentioned anywhere in this book, except in one place where there is a ball rolling down an inclined plane, in which it says how far the ball got after one second, two seconds, three seconds, and so on. The numbers have "errors" in them—that is, if you look at them, you think you're looking at experimental results, because the numbers are a little above, or a little below, the theoretical values. The book even talks about having to correct the experimental errors—very fine. The

trouble is, when you calculate the value of the acceleration constant from these values, you get the right answer. But a ball rolling down an inclined plane, if it is actually done, has an inertia to get it to turn, and will, if you do the experiment, produce five-sevenths of the right answer because of the extra energy needed to go into the rotation of the ball. Therefore, this single example of experimental "results" is obtained from a fake experiment. Nobody had rolled such a ball, or they would never have gotten those results!

"I have discovered something else," I continued. "By flipping the pages at random, and putting my finger in and reading the sentences on that page, I can show you what's the matter—how it's not science, but memorizing, in every circumstance. Therefore I am brave enough to flip through the pages now, in front of this audience, to put my finger in, to read, and to show you."

So I did it. Brrrrrrrup—I stuck my finger in, and I started to read: "Triboluminescence. Triboluminescence is the light emitted when crystals are crushed. . ."

I said, "And there, have you got science? No! You have only told what a word means in terms of other words. You haven't told anything about nature—what crystals produce light when you crush them, why they produce light. Did you see any student go home and try it? He can't.

"But if, instead, you were to write, 'When you take a lump of sugar and crush it with a pair of pliers in the dark, you can see a bluish flash. Some other crystals do that too. Nobody knows why. The phenomenon is called 'triboluminescense.' Then someone will go home and try it. Then there's an experience of nature." I used that example to show them, but it didn't make any difference where I would have put my finger in the book; it was like that everywhere.[*]

Then he offered several examples of students he had met who excelled at parroting definitions of different terms, but who failed miserably when it came to answering questions like "What happens when you crush a lump of sugar with a pair of pliers in the dark?"

The second quote is from *What Do You Care About What Other People Think?*, and is a tribute to Feynman's father/teacher and to spontaneous education. He talks about how his

---

[*]Copyright © W.W. Norton & Company, Inc. (*"Surely, You're Joking Mr. Feynman!"*)

father's habit of taking him out for walks in the woods on weekends had prodded the other fathers in the neighborhood into
doing the same thing. (The fathers typically lived and worked
in New York and were home only on weekends.) Feynman tells
us what happened after one such weekend:

> The next Monday, when the fathers were all back at work, we kids
> were playing in a field. One kid says to me, "See that bird? What
> kind of bird is that?" I said, "I haven't the slightest idea what kind
> of a bird it is." He says, "It's a brown-throated thrush. Your father
> doesn't teach you anything."
>
> But it was the opposite. He had already taught me:
> "See that bird?" he says. "It's a Spencer's warbler." (I knew he
> didn't know the real name.) "Well, in Italian, it's a Chutto
> Lapittida. In Portuguese, it's Bom da Peida. In Chinese, it's
> Chung-long-tah, and in Japanese, it's a Katano Tekeda. You can
> know the name of that bird in all the languages of the world, but
> when you're finished, you'll know absolutely nothing whatever
> about the bird. You'll only know about humans in different places,
> and what they call the bird. So let's look at the bird and see what
> it's doing—that's what counts." (I learned very early the difference
> between knowing the name of something and knowing something.)
>
> He said, "For example, the bird pecks at its feathers all the time.
> See it walking around, pecking at its feathers?"
>
> "Yeah."
>
> He says, "Why do you think birds peck at their feathers?"
>
> I said, "Well, maybe they mess up their feathers when they fly,
> so they're pecking them in order to straighten them out."
>
> "All right," he says. "If that were the case, then they would peck
> a lot just after they've been flying. Then, after they've been on the
> ground a while, they wouldn't peck so much any more—you know
> what I mean?"
>
> "Yeah."
>
> He says, "Let's look and see if they peck more just after they
> land."
>
> It wasn't hard to tell: there was not much difference between the
> birds that had been walking around a bit and those that had just
> landed. So I said, "I give up. Why does a bird peck at its feathers?"
>
> "Because there are lice bothering it," he says. "The lice eat flakes
> of protein that come off its feathers."
>
> He continued, "Each louse has some waxy stuff on its legs, and lit-
> tle mites eat that. The mites don't digest it perfectly, so they emit
> from their rear ends a sugarlike material, in which bacteria grow."

Finally he says, "So you see, everywhere there's a source of food, there's some form of life that finds it."

Now, I knew that it may not have been exactly a louse, that it might not be exactly true that the louse's legs have mites. That story was probably incorrect in detail, but what he was telling me was right in principle.*

Aha! The learning process

"**G**uess which hand it's in," says the little boy, hiding his latest drawing behind his back and waiting for Mom and Dad to coax him into showing it to them. The boy knows that to get his message across, he first has to awaken the curiosity, motivation, and attention of the recipient. For the same reason, we start a conversation with comments like "Guess what happened to me yesterday!" or "This is just plain crazy!" The reaction from the listener is certain: "What happened?" We've made contact.

Our experience has taught us that we need an opening like this before actual communication can start, but we're barely aware of it. It's completely spontaneous, and could be described as an example of "spontaneous teaching."

In the same way, we're receptive to the contents of an instruction manual for a newly purchased product only to the extent that we're interested in getting the product to work. If

---

we're interested, we'll spontaneously decide how to tackle the task at hand. We can call this "spontaneous self-teaching" or, why not, "the spontaneous study method."

With that, I've introduced the first, highly obvious condition for all learning—attention.

Attention in this sense can express itself and be experienced in many different ways: curiosity, excitement, fear, expectation, recognition, hunger, challenge, etc. In formal pedagogy, the term "motivation" is used to signify the same thing. The learning process starts with attention, but what happens then? Let me clarify the description with a simple example.

The woman in the illustrations on page 13 has bought a camera. Her interest in learning to use it has already been aroused; she's curious about how it works, and her curiosity makes her receptive to the information that the camera and the instructions provide. She spontaneously chooses and assimilates the information that is meaningful to her. Just as unconsciously, she ignores other information. The information she takes in is processed in her brain as she uses the trial-and-error method to find meaningful relationships. She continues this way until she understands: "Aha, this is the shutter." Then she tries it a few times just for fun, and to confirm that she has drawn the right conclusions.

This is one way of describing the spontaneous learning process. We can look at the same series of events from other perspectives—some simpler and some much more complicated, but I've found that for our purposes, the previous description is an excellent way to explain spontaneous learning. Here's the learning process in a nutshell:

1. Attention makes us receptive to
2. information, which we
3. process together with prior knowledge, until we arrive at
4. conclusions and understanding, which we then
5. apply and test for confirmation.

This series of mental processes is precisely what film directors, authors, and politicians base their presentations on in order to capture and hold our attention and reach us with their message. Let me give a few more real-life examples that clarify these five terms.

1. Attention: Newspaper headlines, placards, announcements and other advertisements, store signs, and book and record jackets are all examples of things used to attract attention and arouse interest. The same is true of films, novels, and political speeches: the opening is often skillfully designed to capture our interest and make us stay and assimilate the rest. An unusual natural formation, an ancient ruin, or a drop of water hopping around in a hot frying pan can have the same effect. If the conditions are right, our interest will be awakened; our curiosity will be aroused. We're then ready to receive information.

2. Information: But we'll be receptive only if the information meets our expectations to a reasonable degree. If the information is incomprehensible, if there's too much or too little information, or if it's the wrong information, the process will grind to a halt. Newspaper articles are rarely read from beginning to end. We skim an article looking for something meaningful. If we find something, we continue to read or listen. But even if we find information that in itself appears to be meaningful, we still have a distance to go before we achieve real learning, and thus, new knowledge.

3. Processing: The mental processing, the "brainwork," is perhaps the most critical stage. It's in this stage that we compare new and old information. We can see this if we watch people study. They stop reading and look up in order to help the brain look for additional associations. In other words, we spontaneously interrupt our intake of information to give the processing mechanism a chance to work. We can also note how learning tends to continue after a lesson—a sign that the brain is still processing the information and finding new relationships.

4. Conclusion: Relationships are a key factor; the brain is constantly hunting for meaningful relationships, or, to use another expression, gestalts. (According to the definition used in psychology, a gestalt is a "whole" made up of several parts. This "whole" can be an image, a shape, a thought, etc.) It's when such relationships or gestalts become obvious to you that you tend to burst out with an "Aha!" Most of the time, this experience isn't even noticeable, but when it is, it's almost like

The learning process: "She continues until she understands: 'Aha, this is the shutter.' Then she tries it a few times just for fun, and to be sure that she has drawn the right conclusions."

an electric shock running through your body, and you react by sitting up straight as the look of puzzlement vanishes from your face. Even in psychological jargon, this is called "the Aha experience." But with or without these visible or audible manifestations, this is the instant when new knowledge is born.

5. Application: The pleasure we derive in acquiring this new knowledge (insight, understanding, conclusions) drives us on to the next step—to try to apply our knowledge in one way or another. This is the start of a new process, with new learning.

In children, it's often easy to observe each phase in this process. An example: my nine-month-old daughter spots a hammer on the floor. It has attracted her attention, aroused her curiosity. She races to the hammer on all fours, picks it up and examines it. After a period of relative quiet, she starts trying to do different things with it. Finally, she discovers that the hammer is great for banging on the floor. Her success in gaining this insight causes her to break out in a resounding chuckle, after which she confirms her new knowledge with glee and tenacity by making a bunch of small marks on my wood floor.

The learning process doesn't always start as a direct result of external impulses and "outside" information. You've surely noticed how a thought can just "lie there and grow." Sometimes an association initiates a conscious thought process. You search your memory for knowledge/information, and you twist it this way and that until you finally discover relationships you hadn't thought of before.

Without any real outside influence, you've created new knowledge from the knowledge and experiences you already had. Just as often (or probably much more often), this process takes place without your really being aware of it. That's why some people wake up in the middle of the night with the solution to a problem they've had. That's why we can get good ideas in the shower or while skiing down a mountainside. That's why a name you tried in vain to remember suddenly pops into your head much later, in a totally different context.

Your brain simply took matters into its own hands—if you'll excuse the expression—and kept on working on the problem long after you'd given up.

The search for meaning: seeing the big picture

I t's easy to be fascinated by the human trait that drives little people to learn to crawl, walk, and communicate, and big people to scrutinize nature's smallest building blocks in an attempt to figure out how things work.

And we can ask ourselves what's behind this drive.

I won't even try to give a general answer to that question, but there is one characteristic of the brain that is easy to observe, and that has resulted in many interesting conclusions about how we learn: the brain's constant effort to find relationships, to make wholes out of parts, to create gestalts.

This characteristic is worth thinking about, because it holds an important key to understanding how we can improve conditions for learning. With relatively little information, we can use our imaginations to see the "big picture," the gestalt. What we call imagination helps us to interpret the information we receive so that it means something to us. It's hard to *avoid* seeing the square, the circle, and the triangle.

This is one of the fundamental characteristics of our ability to learn—the driving force behind all learning. The pictures below show images of a more traditional kind (taken from psychology textbooks). They also serve as examples of visual gestalts. In these examples it's hard not to see the whole picture, the gestalt. We can't ignore it, even if we try.

These pictures are followed by two more examples where the gestalt is harder to see. It takes some effort. Here's a clue: the first picture contains letters, the second depicts an animal. (You'll find the answers on page 18.)

Even though we can see only a small portion of the letters (below), our brains fill in the missing parts if, and only if, the

We may not have enough information

letters form words and the words form a sentence.
We may not have enough information to determine what an individual letter is, but the context helps us to eliminate all interpretations that lack meaning. One of the two "texts" is meaningful, the other is not. Can you read the message?

Here the brain seems to perform an enormous number of probability estimates in order to arrive at a reasonable interpretation. Of course, this isn't true only for pictures; the same thing happens when we listen.

Here's a simple example.

Suppose you hear someone says "JEETCHET." What does it mean?

You'd probably be confused; your brain wouldn't find a meaningful interpretation.

Now suppose instead that you drop in on friends and find them in the middle of dinner. One of them looks at you, points to the food and says "Jeetchet?" (Did you eat yet?)

I've used this example to illustrate that the brain's way of interpreting and evaluating information depends on several items of information that must be present simultaneously. The most important of these is normally called context. Obviously, prior knowledge and experience are also important. "Jeetchet" out of context is meaningless, but within a context it can be interpreted, and thus, acquires meaning.

Transferred to formal teaching and learning, context can present serious problems. The teacher or textbook author teaches on the basis of his or her understanding of the whole (which is extremely difficult to ignore), while the learner has to rely on the fragments covered so far.

If I start reading a book and come to page 10, I've obviously read only 10 pages.

But when the author wrote page 10, he had already "read the whole book," that is, he had worked out in advance the entire context, the entire gestalt.

What can happen when I read the book is that I either get completely lost, because I can't see the context that the author saw when he wrote it, or I "invent" my own relationships, thereby running the serious risk of drawing the wrong conclusions, which will cause me trouble later on in the book.

At the university level, people are aware of this problem and are discussing ways to reverse the teaching sequence so that instruction starts with a comprehensible overview based on real-life conditions, and then goes into increasingly greater detail. (See Richard Feynman's description in an earlier section.)

This question of context is a central feature of today's teaching and course preparation. I'll have reason to return to it later.

This apparent endeavor of the brain to create gestalts from any available fragments can be called the driving force behind the learning process. It functions spontaneously, but we can facilitate the process with some conscious effort on our part.

It seems reasonable to suppose that this is the same characteristic that gets us interested in things like quiz shows, crossword puzzles, riddles, logic problems, detective stories, and clever nonsense problems in magazines. Their entertainment value lies in their ability to give our activity-hungry brains "something to chew on." The idea is to challenge the brain to work through the process, with the hope of experiencing the pleasure of success that comes with "figuring it out." Here we have a good example of how the learning process can entertain and amuse us.

Narratives of all kinds—stories, films, novels or whatever—entertain us for the same reason. Over and over again, we ask ourselves, "What's going to happen, what's going to happen," as we tensely await the outcome (gestalt). Sports events offer a similar type of entertainment (where the driving force is lost if the final score, the gestalt, is revealed in advance).

The fact that we seek such entertainment is a sign of the brain's efforts to remain active.

We can sum up in the same vein with a riddle: What is it that we do, which we're extremely well-equipped to do, that's fun both while we're doing it and after we've achieved our goal, that demands a minimum of unpleasant effort, and that we use all the time?

Answer: Learning.

Comments on the illustrations on page 16:

1. The picture depicts the word "CARDO" (a company name), but here only the spaces (!) between the letters have been reproduced. The pattern was created by the artist Carl Fredrik Reuterswärd, and is exhibited as a sculpture in the company's lobby.

2. This is a picture of a cow that's looking at you. What's interesting about this picture is that most people can't see the cow, the gestalt, without help. (If you still don't see the cow, you can console yourself with the fact that we'll return to the picture later.)

3. The text: "We may not have enough information"

To learn is to discover

"I'll pay you a million dollars if you can spend a night in the woods, wide awake and without taking drugs, without thinking of a white monkey!" The bet doesn't seem to be especially risky; how could anyone, under these conditions, prevent his or her brain from associating its way to a white monkey at some point during the long night?

You can test your own powers of association: look around the room; look at object after object. Every time you look at an object, say aloud the name of a totally unrelated noun. (For example, look at a chair and say "hamburger.")

Not only is this difficult (after a while you'll be so confused that you may get a stomach ache), but each association will gradually become more closely related to the corresponding object. For example, table-meal, shoe-walk, etc.

We also know very well how a scent, a piece of music, or a face can suddenly evoke memories that have been "buried" for many years.

In the same way, when faced with a new task, we use, often unconsciously, knowledge and skills acquired decades earlier. Not only do we have a fantastic amount of knowledge and experience stored in our brains, but we also have a phenomenal ability to associate (establish relationships) and to quickly find and retrieve from the huge filing cabinet in our heads the information we need.

Faces are a good example.

You go into a department store, your eyes see hundreds of faces, and suddenly your brain detects a relationship between one of these many faces and a memory of a face twenty or thirty years younger. You exclaim, "Well, well, well, if it isn't my old classmate John Jones, the guy who could never sit still in class. . . ."

We can say that research on how the brain works has come far in one sense and not far at all in another. It's come far in that we know much more today than we did only two or three decades ago, and not very far because we have only a very rough idea of how the brain works and how the mechanisms of the brain actually function.

It has been established that different types of mental activity (speech, motor functions, etc.) are concentrated in different parts of the brain.

We know that the right side of the brain controls primarily the left side of the body and vice versa.

There are grounds for concluding that the right side of the brain is more "whole-oriented"—it can see the "big picture," while the left side seems to be best when it comes to details and logic.

We also know that each of our 20 billion brain cells (neurons) is connected to more than 1,000 other brain cells via structures called synapses, and that our brain cells communicate with each other by transmitting electrical impulses through this gigantic network.

Moreover, it seems that once several cells are activated simultaneously, this cell group tends to be easier to activate subsequently.

"Memory" would thus be synonymous with this tendency, and "remembering" would be a subsequent activation of the cells in question.

Finally, when someone says "JEETCHET," the brain starts a searching process, checking all of the impulses that this sound triggers. As part of this searching process, the brain carries out a huge number of "probability estimates," until it finds a reasonable relationship between "jeetchet" and other old and new information: "Aha! He means 'Did you eat yet'!"

The searching process would then be what we call association, and the driving force would be the brain's spontaneous efforts to find relationships, to create gestalts.

What happens in the brain during the learning process can then be explained, using a highly schematic and "mechanical" model like this:

1. Attention can be considered as the activation of groups of brain cells that contain previously recorded experiences, knowledge, or needs.
2. New information related to the information that attracted attention is assimilated and stored temporarily in the brain's short-term memory banks. The new cell groups then activated make contact with those activated earlier.
3. Old and new information is processed in an attempt to find relationships or gestalts. Through association, many cell groups become involved, and more and more connections between cells and cell groups are established. When the brain finds a meaningful relationship, we get a feeling of insight and understanding, a kind of inner experience that activates new cell groups, although this experience is still "wordless" to a certain extent.
4. We use our "intellect" to label the gestalt with an expression or name that will help us handle the new conclusion or knowledge; experience is thereby transformed into knowledge. All of the cell groups involved can thereafter be activated by using this expression or name. This "knowledge unit," or gestalt, is sometimes called a "concept," and the process is called "conceptualization" (the birth of knowledge). Thus, a concept consists of insight, understanding as such, and the name or expression (label). Simple concepts like "chair" mean more or less the same thing to most people, while expressions like "democracy" trigger different associations in different people, depending on how they acquired their knowledge of democracy.
5. When knowledge is used, it acquires additional associations and experiences that reinforce the knowledge and make it even easier to access. (The more cell groups, the more connections.) The knowledge has become part of us; we say that it's been internalized.

This process takes place simultaneously in different dimensions, on different levels of magnification: each step in the learning process consists of all of the other steps, but at a more detailed level. Each step at this more detailed level consists, in turn, of all the steps. (A graphical representation of this internalization process would be a fractal, in which nearly identical patterns are repeated over and over again at different levels of magnification.) The level of magnification we're using here is the one that manifests itself in a learning situation as a path to new, identifiable knowledge, like this:

Mental preparedness and receptiveness.

(Several groups of brain cells are activated.)

Facts and data are converted into information.

(New groups of brain cells are activated and associated.)

Information is converted into experience and insight.

(Associations—the search for meaning. Aha!)

Experience and insight are converted into knowledge.

(A meaningful whole takes shape and becomes a concept.)

Knowledge is converted into skills and attitudes—and wisdom.

(The knowledge acquires more detail and is internalized.)

A "mechanical model" of what happens inside the brain as we learn.

1. Attention. The teacher displays a rectangle: "We know that the area of a rectangle is equal to its length times its width." The teacher draws an arbitrary triangle: "But what is the area of this triangle?"
2. Information. The teacher continues: "If I draw a line like this (draws the height of the triangle), you can see that you get four triangles (fills in the contours of the two rectangles that were formed), each pair of which forms two new rectangles."
3. Processing. "Now let's see if we can figure out what the area of the triangle is." The teacher has created different paths that the learners can follow to reach the conclusion. One learner notes that the sides of the triangle divide the smaller rectangles into two equal parts. Another sees that you can form a new, similar, triangle from the two "cut-off" corners. A third may note both things, and for him or her, one conclusion confirms the other—that the area of the triangle must be half that of the large rectangle.

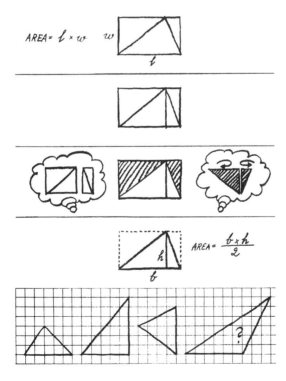

The students learn to calculate the area of a triangle by using their prior knowledge of how to calculate the area of a rectangle.

4. Help in creating knowledge. This "intuitive knowledge" can now be transformed into usable knowledge. The teacher helps: "Yes, that's right; the length times the width divided by two. But here's just one thing: When we talk about a triangle we say height instead of width, and base instead of length. So it's the base times the height divided by two."

5. Confirmation. The participants can then check to see if the formula is valid for other triangles. (Graph paper will help learners to see that they get roughly the same results whether they use the formula or count squares.)

As a result, you know that the area of the triangle is equal to the base times the height divided by two, where the height is the perpendicular distance between the base and the tip of the triangle. (However, the formulation given and the terms used are important only if the knowledge is to serve as the basis for further instruction.)

In this view, the thought process, experience, and conclusions that result from the processing activity in stage three constitute an essential step on the path to new knowledge. But generally, it's the more usable version of the conclusion (stage four) that constitutes true knowledge. Some people feel that the term "learning" should be confined to this transformation of experience into knowledge.

This way of reasoning contains a point that is extremely important for us: suppose you've merely memorized the phrase "The area of a triangle is equal to the base times the height divided by two," without really understanding it. You can recite this phrase if someone asks you how to calculate the area of a triangle, and thus, give the impression that you've acquired new knowledge, but that wouldn't be true. We've all had an experience like this when we were in school.

The same mistake is made in adult education.

T is an instructor. Based on his own experiences and research, he's drawn a number of conclusions and found a suitable way to represent them in a model:

This model then serves as the basis and starting point for a course in business finance. At the end of the course, student S is asked to explain the model, which he does. T then concludes incorrectly that he has transferred knowledge to S, when actually, S has only memorized the labels (the model) without acquiring the underlying experience—the insight. This is like

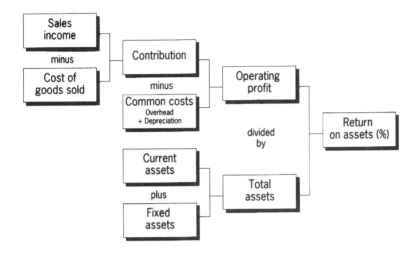

This financial model serves as the basis and starting point for a course in business finance.

learning words in a foreign language without knowing what they mean!

But this is an oversimplification. We often have prior knowledge and experience that enable us to "accept" the model by checking to see whether it constitutes a reasonable description of our own conclusions. The problem with this is that we may think we've understood and learned, even though we haven't. Such experiences are of little value.

A much better way is first to bring our own experiences up to date, and/or find an opportunity to gain new ones (as with the triangles), and then get help in turning these experiences into knowledge by giving them names and perhaps arranging them to form some kind of model. The knowledge acquired will then be richer, contain more associations, and will be more accessible and usable.

And that is exactly how we learn spontaneously. A child points at a kitchen appliance and asks "Da?" ("What's that?"), demanding a name, a label, for his or her experience. This is how all languages develop (including trade jargon).

But we need language for more than just communicating with others. We also need it to "communicate with ourselves," to think. For example, it's important to help children find words/labels for their experiences and feelings at an early age. Parents can do this by asking questions like "Are you disappointed because we didn't go to Grandpa's house?" Words like "disappointed," "angry," "sad," "afraid," and "unsure" are words we need in order to understand and deal with our feelings. In the same way, we need certain words and expressions in order to handle conclusions and insights. With limited language skills at our disposal, we'll have trouble saying what we mean, and this can force us to "mean what we're capable of saying."

On one occasion, I interviewed workers at a large manufacturing company. The questions dealt with their attitudes toward the company, its management, and their jobs. A surprising number of replies consisted of phrases that were strikingly similar to those expressed by the company management in different situations (probably because these respondents thought I represented management), while others were just as similar to the phrases used in the labor union's campaigns (probably because they thought the union had sent me to interview them). It was almost as if I had asked them another question altogether: "What does the company management/labor union think you should think about these matters?"

This happened many years ago, but it still serves to remind me that not even a rich language is a guarantee of correspondingly rich knowledge.

Thus, the quality of knowledge is determined by the many experiences and associations that together make up such knowledge. And training and study are attempts to recreate, in one way or another, the learning process that originally resulted in the knowledge in question. In his book, *The Dancing Wu Li Masters,* Gary Zukav describes his impressions of how an oriental physics instructor teaches:

> A Master teaches the essence. When the essence is perceived, he teaches what is necessary to expand the perception. The Wu Li Master does not speak of gravity until the student stands in wonder at the flower petal falling to the ground. He does not speak of laws until the student, of his own, says, "How strange! I drop two stones simultaneously, one heavy and one light, and both of them reach the earth at the same moment!" He does not speak of mathematics until the student says, "There must be a way to express this more simply."

In this way, the Wu Li Master dances with his student. The Wu Li Master does not teach, but the student learns.*

To learn is to discover.

Competing through learning

Not surprisingly, learning for a company as a whole depends to a great extent on what the competitors come up with. History is full of examples that show that competition is the driving force behind the development of a company's expertise (learning). It seems as though all companies need precisely the same kinds of challenges that we as individuals need in order to grow.

Eric Giertz and Göran Reitberger tell a story from the beginning of this century. It shows that it can be hard to understand in advance the reasons why things later turn out the way they do.

From Lake Ice to the Refrigerator

The first step in the creation of today's household appliance industry was taken at the end of the last century, when a doc-

---

*By permission of William Morrow Co., Inc.

Not even heavy investment in further product development and customer orientation was enough when competitors came up with a new business idea (business logic).

tor at a hospital in the southern United States developed a method for making ice. The doctor needed a way to chill specimens, but lake ice, which had to be brought down from the north, where it was "harvested" from frozen lakes each winter and packed in straw, wasn't always available.

Other doctors and hospitals that needed ice started using the doctor's new ice-making method, and soon word got around, even outside hospitals, that there were machines that could make ice.

At this point, some local firms became interested in the technique and set out to develop more commercial products from the doctor's impractical prototypes. Although machine-made ice was initially much more expensive than lake ice, the scarcity of ice of any kind in the south guaranteed a market for it, albeit a fairly exclusive one. Soon other manufacturers got into the act, offering machines that were better than the first ones. The market grew, and more and more companies entered it. Product development intensified and ice machine prices continued to drop.

It now became clear to the lake-ice dealers up north that the new machines were a real threat, even in the local markets that accounted for most of their sales.

As long as the machines were only sold down south at high prices, the threat to their businesses was marginal. They could even argue that the machines had expanded the market: as more ice was used in the south, the demand for cheap lake ice also increased.

To meet the threat, the lake-ice dealers quickly improved their product in several ways. They started delivering ice in blocks of convenient size, and they introduced tools that made it easy for users to break up the ice into cubes. Delivery men were trained in customer care; they were provided with uniforms and special crates in which to carry the ice into people's kitchens without messing up the floor. Thus, when the suppliers realized that they could no longer compete successfully with machine-made ice on the basis of price alone, they counterattacked by making enormous improvements in customer service, dependability, and efficiency. They succeeded in responding to the new threat with a great deal of creativity and ingenuity.

The strategy was successful to begin with. The ice industry's innovative response to the attack from the ice-machine makers resulted in a dramatic increase in sales of lake ice—from 5 million tons annually in the United States at the time ice machines were introduced, to 15 million tons a few years later, even though machine-made ice captured a substantial share of the market. (The ice industry was not a small-time operation; it employed tens of thousands of people.)

But soon a new threat loomed. New companies emerged from within the ice-machine industry and offered a product that, instead of making ice for refrigeration, provided refrigeration for making ice: the compressor-driven refrigerator. This innovation threatened not only lake-ice suppliers, but even the makers of iceboxes and the fast-growing ice-machine industry.

Once large-scale production of refrigerators with freezer compartments was initiated, the establishment again responded with innovations that greatly enhanced the customer benefits of the traditional technology. Iceboxes were provided with vastly improved insulation and ventilation.

In some of the new models, a given amount of ice lasted three times as long as in older ones. Systems for automatic water drainage were introduced. Service was improved further, and delivery systems became even more customer-oriented. Once more, the establishment succeeded in keeping the new competition at bay for a time, through radical improvements in the traditional system of supplying household refrigeration. But the new technology possessed a development potential that few people could have forseen.

Soon there were many, albeit small, refrigerator manufacturers, and the competition among them spurred product development. Improvements launched by one manufacturer were quickly copied by the others, and the superiority of the refrigerator became increasingly obvious.

As demand increased, the various refrigerator models became more and more alike. The manufacturers then concentrated on rationalizing production methods, cutting production costs, and, as prices dropped, establishing the refrigerator as a mass-market product.

Economies of scale encouraged manufacturers to buy out their competitors, and gradually, the industry was concentrated in the hands of a few big companies—the new establishment. But even before the concentration phase shifted into high gear, the refrigerator had permanently displaced lake-ice cutters, icebox manufacturers, and ice-machine companies into marginal segments of the household refrigeration market.

Actually, the only difference between then and now is the amount of time we have at our disposal—and that's an important difference. For example, how much time can we take to develop a new product and get it into production? Can we take seven years to develop a new car, or do we have to do it in two years? How quickly must we change over to a new production technology? (Today an entire industry may switch from one technology to another within a couple of years, whereas before it could take decades—as in the printing industry.) How long will it take before customers find out that a new product is available? How quickly must we deliver a tailor-made product from a streamlined production system in order to beat our competitors—six months or 24 hours?

We can ask similar questions about capital utilization: is it enough for us to use our plant and equipment eight hours per day, 210 days per year, or do we have to use them 24 hours per day, seven days per week, 365 days per year? How long can we leave products lying around in warehouses?

How long may it take before a person is fully capable of performing his or her job responsibilities?

In the old days, a company had plenty of time. For the most part, it was possible to see what was coming in terms of competition and demand. There was time for a hierarchy of decision makers to plan, control, and check. The people who actually did the work were relegated to the bottom layer of this hierarchy. The main idea behind the industrial organization was to make each job as simple as possible. Now the opposite is true: the ability to see what's coming is highly limited; we no longer have time to wait for decisions and directives from the top. Each and every member of a company must be capable of making necessary decisions within the framework of company-wide aims and objectives. This obviously demands continuous learning on the part of every individual, primarily in three areas.

First, the individual must continuously gain insight into what the business idea really means, so that he or she can determine what conforms and—perhaps more important—what doesn't conform to the business idea.

Second, the individual must remain constantly aware of and evaluate how his or her actions are contributing to the overall operation—how they're helping the company to achieve its goals. This area also includes knowledge of the company's game plan, and an understanding of how rules have to be changed when the company switches from an organization controlled from above, to an organization in which responsibility is delegated. An important factor here is the changing role of staff members: instead of being the reporting (and executive) arm of central decision makers, staff members must serve as consultants for the line functions.

Third, at the very least, the individual must constantly deepen and broaden his or her own expertise.

These are the main areas of what is today called the development of expertise (although activities like outside recruiting and the acquisition of companies are also included here).

One highly interesting question is how continuous learning can be built into a company's operations, or how work can be arranged to stimulate the learning process. (See the depictions of "then" and "now" in the following illustrations.) If the purpose of teaching is to create conditions for learning in a classroom, then the purpose of organization and leadership must be to create conditions for learning within a company (management by learning).

The principles for learning that I discuss in the following chapters are just as valid for learning within a company as they are for learning in a classroom or study situation.

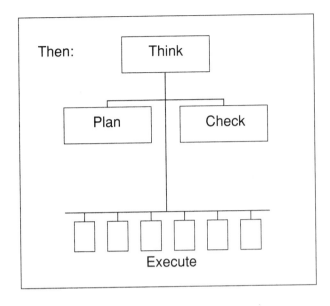

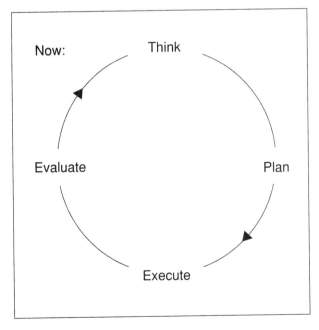

"Then" and "now." Expertise can be developed only if learning (the learning process) is built into each individual's job duties.

2.
The road to knowledge

If you understand the conditions for learning, you can demand more of your learning situation.

Test yourself

When it comes to understanding the conditions for learning, the most important source of knowledge is you; when it comes to your own learning process, no one has more experience than you. But perhaps you still haven't learned to interpret and draw conclusions from your experiences, and to give these conclusions "names" that can guide you when you're taking a course or studying independently.

When we say that there are obstacles to learning, what we're really saying is that the conditions for learning aren't right. We can best illustrate what this means with a concrete example.

We'll start with a learning experiment and we invite you to participate. Its purpose is to illustrate a few major characteristics of formal education that will be easier for you to understand if you have a fresh experience of your own behind you.

Test Your Own Learning

The first test is designed to show how learning can take place. Go through the five parts one by one. Finish each part before going on to the next.

Part 1.

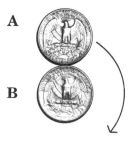

A and B are two coins of equal size. Coin A rolls around the edge of coin B. Coin B doesn't move at all.

Question: When Coin A has rolled all the way around Coin B and returned to its starting point, how many revolutions will Coin A have made around its own center? (Mark your answer.)

❏ One

❏ Two

Part 2. Now let's assume that the correct answer is two. Coin A revolved twice around its own axis. The reason for this is that Coin A does two things at the same time. It not only turns as a consequence of rolling against Coin B, it also makes an additional 360° turn, which amounts to one more revolution. Therefore the answer is two. True or false?

❏ True

❏ False

Part 3. When you replied "true" or "false" in Part 2, did you understand why the correct answer was or was not two turns?

❏ No

❏ I think I understand

❏ I know I understand

Part 4. If you're still unsure of the correct answer, get two coins and try it yourself, until you're certain that you understand. Don't go on until you're completely sure.

Part 5.

C

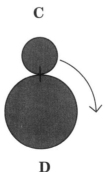

D

Now check the "quality" of your understanding: Coin C is half the size of Coin D. In other words, its diameter, and thus its circumference, are half those of Coin D. Coin C rolls around the edge of coin D. Coin D doesn't move at all.

Question: When Coin C has rolled all the way around Coin D and returned to its starting point, how many revolutions will Coin C have made around its own center? (Mark your answer.)

❑ Two
❑ Three
❑ Four
❑ _____ (more than four)

Comments: The correct answer is three times—two turns because the circumference of Coin D is twice as large, plus one turn because the path of Coin C forms a circle. Before you read on, think for a moment about what helped and what hindered your learning.

Experiences: How you did on this exercise depends on how much time you had available, how interested you were, and your previous experience—in other words, on all of the factors that normally influence learning. Here are some possible outcomes and suggested interpretations. Do you recognize any of them?

❑ You got through all of the exercises without difficulty. (You showed both interest and ability.)
❑ You had to really work, thinking and checking as you went. (You showed both interest and energy.)
❑ You felt the exercise was meaningless and skipped it. (You had neither interest nor expectations.)
❑ You skipped the exercise because you aren't usually very good at such exercises. (You lack self-confidence.)
❑ You gave up after a while because you felt the information was too ambiguous. (You didn't have enough interest to work your way through the ambiguity in the information.)
❑ You knew the answers before you started. (You lacked interest because you had nothing to gain.)
❑ You cheated by skipping the exercises and peeking at the answers. (You had a certain amount of curiosity, but not enough to actually do the exercises.)

❑ You still don't understand, even though you remember the answers "two times" and "three times." (You remember, but you haven't learned.)

Many people mix up "remembering" and "understanding" in the context of learning.) But what's most interesting about the previous list is that it serves as an inventory of how most of us normally react in different kinds of learning situations.

Let's return to the model of the learning process and try to find out what the most common obstacles are—what it is that's of critical importance in each of the five steps. Let's do this with the help of a test like the one you just finished. You can use it to test whatever is normally most critical for you.

On the following pages you'll find 11 short texts (articles, descriptions, explanations) of different kinds. They're similar in some ways to the type of information normally provided in many companies' training materials, but here they've been modified to serve as simple illustrations of different conditions for learning. These texts are followed by a series of questions—in the form of a knowledge test—and thereafter by comments that include fairly general conclusions about the conditions for learning.

You can use these examples to find out for yourself what it is that influences your learning process.

Examples

Instructions:

1. Read and study the texts and pictures on the following pages for 15 to 20 minutes.

2. Then find out how much you really learned by answering the questions on pages 50 to 53.

20 min.

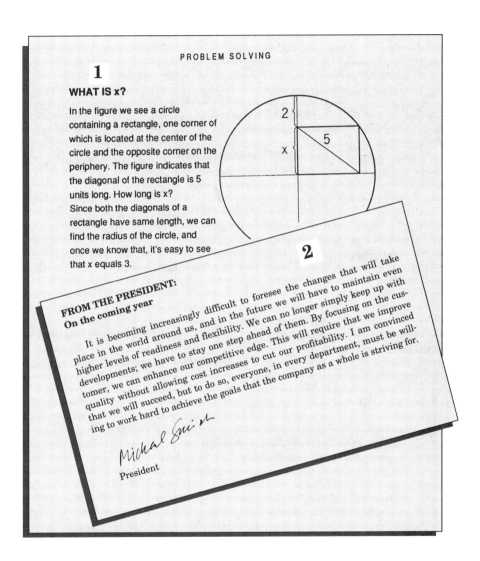

PROBLEM SOLVING

1

WHAT IS x?

In the figure we see a circle containing a rectangle, one corner of which is located at the center of the circle and the opposite corner on the periphery. The figure indicates that the diagonal of the rectangle is 5 units long. How long is x? Since both the diagonals of a rectangle have same length, we can find the radius of the circle, and once we know that, it's easy to see that x equals 3.

2

FROM THE PRESIDENT:
On the coming year

It is becoming increasingly difficult to foresee the changes that will take place in the world around us, and in the future we will have to maintain even higher levels of readiness and flexibility. We can no longer simply keep up with developments; we have to stay one step ahead of them. By focusing on the customer, we can enhance our competitive edge. This will require that we improve quality without allowing cost increases to cut our profitability. I am convinced that we will succeed, but to do so, everyone, in every department, must be willing to work hard to achieve the goals that the company as a whole is striving for.

Michael Smith

President

3

RHETORIC

The classical art of public speaking (rhetoric) offers a wealth of models and concepts on how an effective speech should be structured. Here's an example of the key feature of a good speech.

The EXORDIUM (introduction) is designed to awaken interest and give the audience a favorable impression of the speaker, and to provide the audience with a glimpse of the subject and nature of the speech.

This is followed by the NARRATIO, the subject of the speech. It can take the form of a description or a narrative.

The next stage is called the PROPOSITIO. Here the speaker presents a conclusion or hypothesis that can be tested intellectually.

In the ARGUMENTATIO, rational arguments are presented to support the conclusion.

The speech concludes with the PERORATIO, a summary whose purpose is to persuade people to take action.

4

THE ART OF KILLING CROWS
How to rid your yard of crows

"First, make paper cones and coat the insides with bird glue. Place a piece of raw meat inside and insert the cones in the ground or in the snow wherever the crows gather. When the crow attempts to pick up the meat with its beak, the cone gets stuck on its head, preventing it from seeing. Its normal reaction is to fly straight up into the air as high as it can. It then falls back to the ground and is usually killed."
(From Sven Nilsson's book entitled "The Fauna of Scanidaniva")

Pictures create many associations, so it's easier to remember a series of pictures if they have something in common, like these.

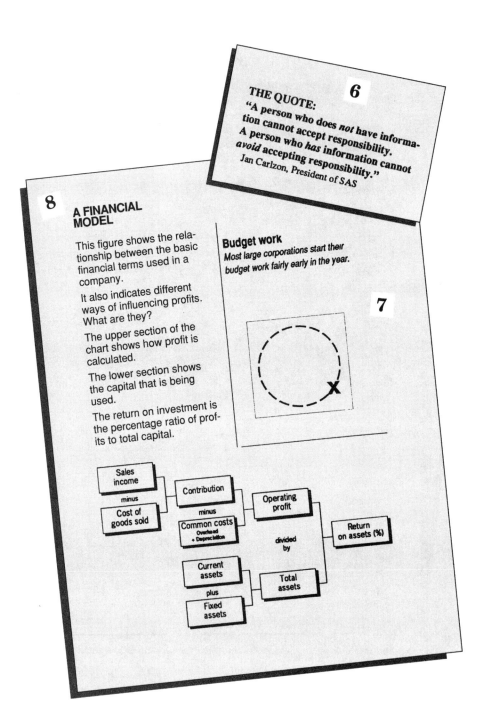

6

A FINANCIAL MODEL

8

This figure shows the relationship between the basic financial terms used in a company.

It also indicates different ways of influencing profits. What are they?

The upper section of the chart shows how profit is calculated.

The lower section shows the capital that is being used.

The return on investment is the percentage ratio of profits to total capital.

Budget work
Most large corporations start their budget work fairly early in the year.

7

Sales income

minus

Cost of goods sold

Contribution

minus

Common costs
Overhead + Depreciation

Operating profit

divided by

Return on assets (%)

Current assets

plus

Fixed assets

Total assets

9

The Portrait

This riddle has become a classic:

A man (A) points at a photo and says: "This man's father is my father's only son." Who's in the picture?

Since we're talking about "this man's father," the picture cannot be of man A himself. But the brain could have trouble keeping the various lines of reasoning separated, and we can easily conclude (incorrectly) that the man is pointing to a picture of himself.

10

The brain is always striving to create meaningful "wholes." Even if you only have a few parts of a figure to work with, your brain fills in the missing parts. Such a whole is called a *gestalt*.

Thoughts

The comic strip is an example of a gestalt – an idea, a thought, a concept. But the gestalt isn't complete; we've hidden the last line. *What did Tiger's little brother say? How would you finish the line?*

Pictures

This figure is another example of an incomplete gestalt.
Can you see the cow in the picture?

HOW MANY MATCHES?

11

A single-round elimination tennis tournament for 10 players will be held. See the playing schedule to the right here. At the end of the tournament there will be one victor and nine losers. Nine matches will be played, the same number as the number of losers. This is confirmed by the playing schedule.

Questions

Here is a series of questions about the 11 examples on the preceding pages.

How much did you learn?

Then look at the comments and conclusions on pages 53 to 64.

1. WHAT IS *x*?

A. How long is *x*?

ANSWER: _____

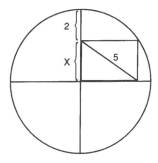

B. Here's a similar exercise: In the figure, we see a square drawn within another square drawn within a circle. The side of the small square is seven units long. What's the radius of the circle?

ANSWER: _____

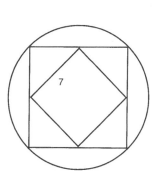

2. FROM THE PRESIDENT

What is the company president trying to say in his letter? What was the most important message?

ANSWER: _____

_____

3. RHETORIC

What are the five stages of rhetoric mentioned in the text?

ANSWER: _____

_____

_____

_____

4. THE ART OF KILLING CROWS

The text describes a method for getting rid of crows. Make an instructional drawing to accompany the text.

ANSWER:

5. THREE PHOTOGRAPHS

What do these three pictures have in common?

ANSWER: _____

_____

6. THE QUOTE

What point is Jan Carlzon trying to make in his statement about responsibility?

ANSWER: _____

7. BUDGET WORK
The caption for the picture reads, "Most large corporations start their budget work fairly early in the year." Roughly which month was meant?

ANSWER: _____

8. A FINANCIAL MODEL
How is profitability (Return On Assets) affected in the following cases, assuming everything else remains the same? Indicate your answer with a plus or minus sign as shown in the example.

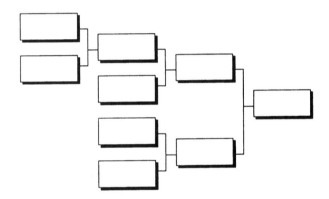

What happens to profitability when:

- the cost of goods sold declines? (+)

- the gross profits increase? ( )

- current assets decrease? ( )

- income increases? ( )

- total assets increase? ( )

- the price goes up? ( )

- the capital tied up in fixed assets increases? ( )

9. THE PORTRAIT
The man points at the picture and says "This man's father is my father's only son." Who appears in the photo? Explain the logic behind your answer.

ANSWER: _____

_____

10. VISUAL GESTALTS
Ideas:
What idea or thought was the comic strip trying to illustrate?

ANSWER: _____

Images:
Make a drawing of the cow you see in the picture.

ANSWER:

11. HOW MANY TENNIS MATCHES?
A. A single-round elimination tennis tournament with ten players will be held. How many matches will be played?

ANSWER: _____

B. Another tennis tournament will be held with 100 players. How many matches will be played?

ANSWER: _____

Conclusions

What was your reaction to this learning experiment? The exercise was used in courses about learning, and there we observed a wide range of attitudes toward it. Here are some examples:

1. a chance to test brainpower.
2. little inclination to get involved ("Come to the point instead!")
3. suspicion—the person doesn't really want to know, or is afraid of being tricked into revealing something

So the person's initial attitude sets the limits for how much he or she can get out of the assignment. This in itself is an important lesson. The reactions to the individual exercises also vary widely. Some examples:

- I hate math problems.
- Exercises like this one make me nervous.
- I knew this before.
- Meaningless knowledge isn't worth wasting energy on.
- I remember the answer, but I never really understood it.
- I had trouble concentrating.
- I didn't spend enough time on it.
- That's not my field.
- It was interesting, so it was easy.
- I just plain didn't give a damn whether I could do it or not.
- It's harder to learn than you think.
- It's easier to learn than you think.

Here are the "correct" (expected) answers, and an attempt to interpret the main types of obstacles that occur in formal instruction and learning. (We say "attempt" because in practice, the number of possible interpretations is infinite.)

1. WHAT IS x?

A: From the description alone, we can deduce that x equals 3. (Many people fail to notice that the diagonals are equal, and instead try to use the Pythagorean Theorem, which won't work.)

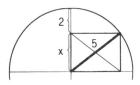
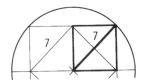

The diagonal = the radius = 5.

Thus, $x = 5 - 2 = 3$.

The diagonal of the small square = the radius = 7.

B: The diagonals in the dashed square have a length of 7, so the radius of the circle is also 7. If you understood the answer to the first problem, you can apply the same "idea" to solve the second problem. See the figure.

Your score:
❑ I failed.
❑ I answered question A but couldn't answer question B.
❑ I answered both questions (learned now or knew before).

But the interesting question is whether you bothered to try to solve the problems at all because you're simply not interested in math problems of this kind, or because you have a mental block resulting from bad experiences with such problems in the past. ("I just can't do problems like these.") I've noted that several of the other exercises produce the same reaction.

Conclusion: People who believe in their own abilities are usually proven right. The same is true of those who don't.

It's surprising how many people have mental blocks to learning caused by unpleasant past experiences.

2. FROM THE PRESIDENT

Obviously, this is a trick question, and an especially tricky one at that. But if we assume that the president clearly knows what must be done, then his efforts are even more tragic because his letter doesn't give the reader a single clue.

Your score:
❑ I didn't remember anything.
❑ I thought I found one main message.
❑ I realized that the message was completely ambiguous.

When an announcement containing contradictory messages is issued within a company, the reader usually manages to "see" one of the messages—the one that agrees best with other signals from the company's management. If investments, advertising, etc., show that management is serious (or not serious) about focusing on the customer and improving quality, then that's what the reader reads into the text.

Conclusion: A message must be free from contradictions before it can communicate ideas.

Naturally, problems also occur when the message is unambiguous ("Our people are our most important resource"), but management's actions demonstrate just the opposite.

In such cases, actions always speak louder than words. I've observed parents giving their teenagers a last word of advice on a Friday evening. Leaning forward and pointing a cautioning index finger in the air, they say sharply "And remember—I trust you!" Obviously, the message the youths receive is the exact opposite, and if the parents use this tactic in many different situations, the young people may simply conclude that their parents don't trust them.

This is an example of meta-learning (*meta* = beyond). It goes on all the time. It's not unusual for a lecturer and author to talk down to his students, to treat them as "less knowledgable" beings. The risk here is that the only lesson the students will learn is that "I'm not considered qualified." Or what about the student who was asked, "What was the most important thing you learned in your economics course?" He replied, "Well, I learned that economics is horribly dull." "Didn't you learn anything else?" "Yeah, I also learned that I really didn't know what I thought I knew."

3. RHETORIC

Correct answers:
   EXORDIUM
   NARRATIO
   PROPOSITIO
   ARGUMENTATIO
   PERORATIO

Your score:

❑ I didn't remember anything.
❑ I remembered some of the technical words.
❑ I learned (or already knew) the thought process and the technical words.

This is a tough exercise. For a lot of people, it doesn't mean anything. That's why the material is hard to remember and to learn. In addition, it includes a number of strange words that probably have little meaning for the reader. (Actually, it was a little unfair of us to purposely present this interesting subject in such a boring way.)

Conclusion: Before learning can take place, the form and content of the information have to correspond to an aim, an interest, or a need on the part of the recipient.

But we've found that in spite of the inherent difficulties, many people manage to understand the idea that the author is trying to get across, and to see the similarities between the material and the five steps in the learning process. They learn something about the subject, perhaps without paying much attention to the labels ("exordium," "narratio," etc.). So a "test of knowledge" that asks for the names of these technical words would incorrectly indicate that the test taker hadn't learned anything.

On the other hand, if the test taker succeeds in naming the five technical words, does that automatically mean that he or she has learned? Of course not. And this is a common mistake in traditional education, where learning is still often evaluated this way.

4. THE ART OF KILLING CROWS

Your score:

- ❏ I failed completely.
- ❏ I remembered vaguely.
- ❏ I learned the method.

You probably remember the instructions, perhaps even in detail, because the cruelty of this method of killing crows made such a powerful impression on you. The new term "bird glue" (whatever that is) also tends to help people remember.

Conclusion: How much we learn also depends on how strongly we're impressed (positively or negatively) by the presentation.

In addition, what we learn from this exercise depends on the context in which it is presented. In his book, *On the Art of Reading and Writing,* Olof Lagercrantz discusses the passage cited here and contends that another heading would have given the text another meaning. If the heading were changed to "The danger of being blinded by career ambitions and the lust for power," our interpretation of the text, and thus, our conclusions, and what we learn, would be completely different.

5. THREE PHOTOGRAPHS
This exercise leads us to the same considerations as the one above about crows. Here are three common results:

1. You remember the pictures (or a couple of them), but you see no connection between them.
2. You seem to remember that there are three objects in each picture.
3. You see in the pictures different types of health and environmental hazards.

Your score:

❑ I don't remember them at all.
❑ I remember the pictures, but found nothing in common.
❑ I remember the pictures and found something in common—the environment.

The last interpretation is the most common, so let me talk about that one. The interesting question here is how people in the early 1960s would have reacted to the same pictures:

1. The factory smoke shows that industry is thriving and that the country is flourishing.
2. At that time, smoking was a symbol for freedom and independence. (Remember that the link between smoking and lung cancer wasn't made public until well into the 1960s. Before that, one could even see ads where doctors talked about the benefits of their favorite brand of cigarettes, and children reading Donald Duck comics were invited to figure out how many cigars Donald, Scrooge McDuck, and Gladstone Gander smoked altogether.)
3. The high-rise apartment complex was viewed as a welcome symbol of the battle against housing shortages and slums.

In the 1960s, these were three examples of well-being and progress. Today, they are three examples of threats to well-being and progress.

Look at this exercise symbolically. We interpret all information against the background of our own values, experiences, and knowledge. When, as in the example, the time span is 30 years, the results are perhaps more striking, but this phenomenon is present to a great extent in all learning situations. An example at the other end of the spectrum is our view of the term "productivity." It's highly likely that an assembly line supervisor has learned over his entire working life that productivity means maximum utilization of machinery and labor.

So when a company starts teaching different methods of increasing dependable delivery and reducing tied-up capital, there are many messages that conflict with the supervisor's basic attitudes and experience. Here, teaching and learning take place in two different conceptual worlds (paradigms), and the result will be lack of understanding, lack of learning, and a tinge of mistrust. It's even more serious when a bad experience causes the learner to lose faith in the knowledge that he or she already had. This is called "negative learning."

My experiences have convinced me beyond a shadow of a doubt that the effectiveness of training can increase dramatically if, above all, we help participants to examine and reappraise their conceptual worlds, and thus make them more receptive to alternatives. Only then should we delve into the matter of what the consequences of a change in attitudes can be. Trying to proceed in the reverse order (which is more common) can be a slow, difficult, and frustrating process.

Conclusion: Our experiences and values change over time, and they influence the way we interpret and evaluate the information we receive.

6. THE QUOTE

Interpreted in one way, Jan Carlzon's quote is quite trivial: "You need information before you can accept responsibility." But this interpretation doesn't tell the whole story, because Carlzon goes much further: the person who has information automatically accepts responsibility. He or she doesn't need to be urged to accept responsibility, and doesn't have to be supervised or monitored in any traditional way. This notion has far-reaching implications.

Your score:

❑ I don't remember anything.
❑ I remember that it was about information and responsibility.
❑ I thought about what the text really means (as discussed in the preceding paragraph).

Quotes like this one often illustrate significant insights and attitudes concisely, but they can easily turn into "empty words," because we tend to interpret things within the framework of what we can do and what we really believe. For example, many companies formulate a "mission," "vision," or "business idea," and then stress how important it is that everyone truly understand it. But we seldom get any help in interpreting what it means for us in practical terms—especially when it comes to taking action and making decisions in our daily work. The absence of such help results in a broad range of possible interpretations, and we naturally choose the one that gives the meaning that benefits us most. So we really haven't learned anything.

Conclusion: We tend to interpret other people's conclusions in the way that best meets our own expectations and needs.

7. BUDGET WORK
Most people would say April or May without hesitation. That shows how strong our visual memory is.

Your score:

❑ I don't remember.
❑ I couldn't remember without looking at the picture.
❑ I thought about it and decided that the picture could be interpreted in different ways.

But some people just don't see the year that way, as a circle with January 1 at the top (12 o'clock) and with time moving clockwise. There are many other ways to imagine a year, and some of them are shown in the illustrations.

This example demonstrates that sometimes we automatically assume that everybody thinks exactly the way we do, and that this isn't always the case.

Conclusion: Different people create different images of abstract concepts.

That's why it can be frustrating at times to be "forced" into accepting other people's imagery and metaphors. Management and leadership literature tends to be full of such devices, but quite often they don't work as intended—as aids in systematizing the reader's understanding. Charts of different kinds also provoke resistance in some people, even if the author has worked hard to keep them simple. One single type of imagery simply isn't suitable for everyone. More about this in the following example.

8. A FINANCIAL MODEL

The correct answers, assuming that all other factors remain the same, are ("+" = profitability increase; "–" = profitability decreases):

- decrease in costs   (+)
- increase in gross margin   (+)
- decrease in current assets   (+)
- increase in income   (+)
- increase in total assets   (–)
- price increases   (+)
- increase in capital tied up in fixed assets (–)

Your score:

- ❑ I didn't try or failed.
- ❑ The model meant nothing to me.
- ❑ I knew all the answers (learned now or knew before).

Some teaching methods require that the student already know the material being taught. This exercise is an example of a "model." Models like these are used in all conceivable (and sometimes inconceivable) situations to illustrate different kinds of relationships, and they often constitute an important intellectual aid to learning. If you fully understood the model and the concepts contained in it, you won't have any trouble answering all of the questions we asked above. If you didn't understand it, some of the questions will be harder to answer.

I've already commented on this example in an earlier section, but I'd like to repeat what I said then. The teaching process, or you as a student, must try to recreate the learning process that resulted in the model. Studying the model won't help you if you don't possess the underlying experience and understanding.

Conclusion: The primary function of theoretical models is to help people organize the experiences and insights they already have.

This is extremely important, because different people have different ways of gaining insight. Some need to start with practical, concrete examples, while others prefer more abstract lines of reasoning to avoid getting bogged down in details.

9. THE PORTRAIT

So who's the man in the portrait? Is it the man himself, his son, or his father? Hint: There's only one possible answer.

Your score:

❑ I didn't try or failed.
❑ I think I know the answer.
❑ I know the answer (figured it out or knew before).

There's a similarity between this exercise and the one about the two coins. It's not enough for somebody to tell us the answer; we have to think through the problem ourselves and arrive at our own understanding before we can achieve real learning, and thus knowledge.

Conclusion: Genuine learning requires an effort on our part to achieve genuine understanding. Learning demands thinking.

Back in the 1970s, when I was training instructors, I often used this exercise about the portrait to illustrate how some teaching methods tend to cause more problems than they solve. I divided the participants into groups, and to arouse interest, I said "Now let's see which group finishes first." But there was a catch: "finished" meant that everyone in the group understood the reasoning behind the group's collective answer, and that each person in the group was capable of proving to me that he or she really understood. This exercise could take hours. As soon as one group member thought he or she had solved the problem, this person immediately proceeded to "teach" the others in the group. Symbolic portraits were displayed, and no effort was spared in trying to persuade the others to understand the solution. The "students" often nodded in agreement, but remained totally confused. The more confused the "students" became, the more ammunition in the "teacher's" explanations. There was no trace of what I'd hoped they'd learned in the course on conditions for learning. Of the people who were most confused, vague attempts to get some help from those who had already understood the solution immediately resulted in a new cascade of explanations, and in a few cases, when there was only one person left to persuade, the straggler would literally shout (with a great deal of insight): "Just shut up and let me figure it out for myself!"

On a similar occasion at a large American company, my otherwise appreciative host got extremely frustrated at one point and asked me straight out whether what we were doing was a reasonable way to use the time at our disposal. I parried by saying, "I'm ready to go on like this all week if necessary; otherwise, what was the point of starting in the first place?" Of course, I was deliberately being provocative, but the conclusion we both drew a while later was the following:

Don't include anything in the course material unless you intend to give the participants the time and opportunity they need to understand and learn. Include only things that are really important, and then give these things the attention they deserve.

As a result, many of the courses currently being offered were eliminated.

Or, as a customer once said to me, "Before, we managed to show 68 overheads in a half a day: With your methods, we're lucky if we can get through three in a whole day. What kind of effectiveness is that?" Obviously, the question here is what you use for a yardstick. What counts, the number of information units presented per hour, or the number of people that have understood and learned?

10. VISUAL GESTALTS
Your score:

❏ I didn't remember anything.
❏ I remembered what the strip was about but didn't know the message.
❏ I knew what both the strip and the message were about.

The comic strip about Tiger and his dog was presented earlier in the book. How did you react when you saw it this time? What can happen is that the first time we see an analogy like this one, it confirms something we already knew or believed. But later, once we've acquired more relevant experience, the same allegory suddenly increases in value because it also serves as an expression of our newly attained insights.

Conclusions: New information sometimes helps to confirm and reinforce "what we already knew."

This is what the cow looks like. Once you've previously encountered it, it's practically impossible not to see it.

Your score:

❏ I didn't see the gestalt at all.
❏ I thought I saw a cow somewhere else in the picture.
❏ I saw the cow and could draw the main features.

Think of this example as a reminder that we sometimes need help in seeing the whole, the gestalt, when we have only a number of unrelated elements of knowledge to go on. In lectures, I sometimes use this picture as a symbol for education at the university level. Over several years, students learn fragment after fragment after fragment. Only much later, when they're out practicing their professions, do some of them manage to grasp the whole—to "see the cow."

Conclusion: We sometimes need help in seeing certain

gestalts.

From my own years in school, I especially remember how lengthy, complicated, and obscure mathematical proofs concluded with a laconic "from which we can easily deduce that $A = B$." This was not especially encouraging or especially helpful.

11. HOW MANY TENNIS MATCHES?

A: If there are 10 tennis players, there will be 9 matches.

B: If there are 100 tennis players, there will be 99 matches. In other words, the number of matches is the same as the number of losers in the tournament.

Your score:

❑ I failed completely.
❑ I answered question A but not question B.
❑ I learned now or knew before.

If you answered question B correctly, then you probably accept the conclusion that the number of matches is equal to the number of players minus one, or the number of losers. Many people answer 90 to question B, which means that they've drawn the wrong conclusion. But others who succeeded in answering question B correctly can be stumped if the number of players is changed to, say, 498.

So here we can see the entire range of understanding, from "remembering the conclusion" to "refusing to believe it's true, even if it happens to be true in these specific examples" to "understanding and accepting the conclusion."

This shows that if we don't get a chance to check the validity and relevance of what we think we've understood (learned), then the knowledge isn't worth very much. Only when an arranger of a tennis tournament has to draw up schedules and reserve courts for a competition with 1,261 players will the validity (the quality) of this knowledge be put to the test. Does he or she dare to trust in this knowledge and the conclusion that the number of matches to be played is 1,260?

Conclusion: Before we can believe in and use new knowledge, we have to confirm its validity through experience.

We can call this process internalizing.

Obstacles

N ow we can relate the obstacles discussed in the examples to the learning process and to its various phases in order to get a more general overview of the most common obstacles to learning, and where in the process these obstacles arise.

1. **The first conditions for learning are attention, curiosity, and interest. Here are typical obstacles:**
   - The instruction simply has no meaningful objective.
   - The objective of the instruction is hard to discern.
   - The learner lacks a meaningful objective.

   Examples: 1. what is x?, (and several others).

2. **With regard to information, the most common obstacles are:**
   - The information is inconsistent and contains contradictory messages.
   - Different frames of reference give the information different meanings.
   - Wrong form—too theoretical, little relation to real-life conditions, boring.
   - Complicated language.
   - Obscure terminology.
   - Presented in the wrong order.

   Examples: 2. From the President, 3. Rhetoric, 4. The Art of Killing Crows, 5. Three Photographs, 6. The Quote.

3. **The learner must process the information before he or she can transform it into experience and draw conclusions. The obstructions in the processing stage are things like:**
   - Lack of time.
   - Lack of substance, of material to be processed.
   - No relation or unclear relation between the exercises and the objective.
   - Wrong form.

Examples: 7. Budget Work, 8. A Financial Model, 9. The Portrait.

4. **The learner will be unable to transform experiences and intuitive conclusions into useful knowledge if:**
   - The suggested conclusion (knowledge) conflicts with the learner's intuitive conclusion.
   - The gap between the learner's frame of reference and the knowledge is too wide.
   - The form of the knowledge (model, formulation) is perceived as unsuitable.
   - The learner gets no help at all in turning his or her intuitive insights into intellectual knowledge (a process we call conceptualization).

   Example 10. Gestalts

5. **Application and usefulness, which reinforce knowledge, require:**
   - The transfer of the knowledge acquired in the classroom to the situation in which it is to be used.
   - The opportunity to use (test) the knowledge in the intended context.

   Example: 11. How Many Tennis Matches?

The dream obviously is to modify the training process in a way that eliminates all of these obstacles. But what should we as learners do while we're waiting for this dream to come true? Up to now, we've been forced to accept the obstacles, to struggle through them, and make the best of the situation. But it doesn't have to be that way. Even when the circumstances seem to be unfavorable, there are many things the individual can do to avoid falling victim to them. Here are two of them.

The first is to encourage a continuous dialogue between learners and instructors so that, working together, they can improve the training process and create better conditions for learning. The second is to apply your own learning methods to the training methods being used. Clearly, both of these measures are necessary.

ground, training, and interests. These differences in results confirm the importance of not designing instruction for some sort of "typical student," because there is no such thing as a typical student. In spite of this, instruction has for many years been planned and designed for a "typical student" within a "target group." Here, it's been assumed that the other students in the group are distributed around the "typical student" following a normal curve, and attempts have been made to create elements of "individualization" to cope with the differences. If we look at things strictly logically, and imagine that knowledge can be quantified (measured in units), the assumption described above is appropriate. But we're moving toward a new way of looking at things, where knowledge is evaluated qualitatively. That's why people in many places are in the process of revising the form and content of even the most basic training concepts and searching for new ways to evaluate the results and effects of the instruction being offered.

A new, fundamental view of education is taking shape. One interesting question in passing is whether the groups' results would have been more uniform if, instead of participating in a voluntary experiment, the subjects had been studying for a test whose outcome determined whether they'd get a pay raise, for instance. I believe so because external motivators like grades, salary, or threats can make us "study harder." The problem is that knowledge acquired this way is generally much less useful (and the learning process is much less enjoyable). But, as I intend to demonstrate, there are ways to avoid "cramming," even under circumstances of this kind.

In front of me I see 28 small bodies squirming around in their seats. The teacher is up at the front, safely facing the blackboard, where she's drawing what appears to be a tiny square, mumbling that. . .

". . .sincetheareaofarectangleisequaltothelengthtimesthewidhtandthelengthandwidthofasquareareequaltoeachotherandarecalledsidestheareaofasquareisequaltothelengthofonesidetimes itself. . . .

Got that?!

I observed this scene just a little over ten years ago, when I was invited to "open house" at my childrens' school. And it was disheartening. More than anything else, it reminded me of my own years in school. Is this, I wondered, how we as children acquire the behavior we display as adults at courses and lectures? Is this where we learn how students and teachers are supposed to behave?

I personally can't imagine a more unfavorable environment for learning than a room of the type where courses are traditionally held. It's bare, completely void of anything that could help to create associations. The only window to reality in the room is an overhead projector, and the person we call the instructor alone decides how much reality should be allowed to enter through this window, and how it should be depicted. Overhead after overhead, with text, circles, squares, and arrows in different arrangements that we call models. And just as some of the people (those lucky enough to be sitting sufficiently close to the front to see what was written on the overhead) start to make some sense out it, the overhead is removed to make room for the next one. The conditions for learning are dictated by the instructor.

Or, in the words of an anecdote from the bygone days of the little red schoolhouse:

- Well, children, have you learned anything today?
- No, teacher, we've been too busy listening to you.

I'm often criticized for this description of education. "It's unfair," they say, "and even offensive. That's not the way it is—at least not any more." They feel that this description is an insult to all competent teachers and lecturers.

I can agree with the last part. It's just that the teachers and lectures I would describe as competent are still in a minority. And I'm not basing that on my status as a professional educator, but on my fairly long experience as an adult student, where the several extremely rewarding experiences I've had have merely served to point out the deficiencies of the many poor ones.

This is a touchy subject. Many people perceive criticism of their teaching ability as a personal attack. Another indication that this is a sensitive matter is the docility that people with otherwise strong personalities can display when they find themselves in the role of course participant. They sit there without protesting, allowing many hours of their time to be wasted, and then, at the end of the course, they (possibly) indicate their dissatisfaction by offering a negative evaluation. But then it's too late. So we have to ask ourselves whether it isn't the course participants themselves that are mostly to blame. I personally believe that this is true to some extent.

A Typical Situation

The participants are working in groups. The instructor approaches the members of one group to find out how they're doing. The group leader turns to the instructor and says: "Was this the way you wanted it?" For whose benefit are they doing the assignment anyway?

Or, "I didn't understand a thing during the past two hours." "Why didn't you say something?" "Well, I didn't want to interrupt you while you were teaching."

Sometimes I get the feeling that students behave as if they were there only to give the instructor an excuse to show his or her overheads.

So rather than embark on a witch-hunt of teachers, I think it would be more constructive to examine and challenge the traditional notions that lie behind the ways we teach and the ways we allow ourselves to be taught—to view these notions in light of the demands that modern adult students, more aware of their own needs, are starting to make in terms of what should be taught and how it should be taught. We should challenge the long-standing idea that education is a collection of rituals.

What I'm looking for is better interaction between instructors and students in the training process. We need an atmosphere of cooperation where the people involved abandon their rituals and roles as traditional teachers and equally traditional students—roles that none of them really want! These undesirable role expectations, constantly reinforcing each other, are the prime cause behind the low level of effectiveness in formal education.

A student's reflection:
Because the teacher behaves,
the way he thinks I think he should behave,
perhaps I behave,
the way I think he thinks I should behave,
even though neither of us wants to behave,
the way either of us is behaving!

The new learner

The economic climate of the past few years has been one of the major forces behind the renaissance in education. Demands for greater effectiveness and more efficient use of resources are forcing people to search for alternatives to today's teaching methods. Reviews of teaching methods and ways of working haven't been included in all of the austerity measures being adopted, but where they have been included, it has been because the students and their supervisors are demanding more learning out of less teaching.

Here we can illustrate the "traditional student" and the "modern student" by showing how two people thank their instructors at the end of a one-week course.

Della: I just want to thank you for a fabulous course. Ralph and the other instructors have done a fantastic job. You've been terrific. The course was excellent, useful, and instructive, and I'm sure that once we get home and have a chance to absorb everything, we'll benefit enormously from what we've learned. I'm sure all of the others agree with me.

(Then Harry gets up, somewhat cautiously. He too has something to say.)

Harry: Look, I'm sorry, but I have to disagree. I imagine Ralph would be disappointed if he knew how little I've learned over the past week. This course has made me feel stupid, incompetent, and incapable, even though I know Ralph really made an effort. He did the best he could, but the question is whether we did the best we could. What I've finally realized is that if I'm going to learn anything, I'm going to have to draw my own conclusions based on my own experiences. In other words, I have to be involved, really involved.

How can two people have such differing impressions of the same events? Are they talking about the same course? Clearly, the difference is that they've evaluated their experiences in totally dissimilar ways. Most likely, they're both talking about an ordinary, well-run course (or seminar, conference, training program, or whatever you want to call it). We're all quite familiar with the model: the instructor did what he or she was expected to do, the students did what they were expected to do, and at the end of the course, a few kind words to confirm that the course was worthwhile. The course has fulfilled the norms, everyone gives him or herself and all of the others a passing grade, and they all go home, pleased with their efforts.

But looking at the course from a different point of view, the description is the exact opposite. "I feel stupid, incompetent, and incapable," says Harry, revealing that his demands—not least on himself—were completely different. He's irritated because everyone expected so little, and he's disappointed because he let himself fall so easily into the traditional role of student. "I have to draw my own conclusions based on my own experiences," he says, when at last he realizes how much time he's wasted over the past week.

After this provocative introduction, Harry continues to tell the others what he learned from not learning. He talks about his experiences over the past week, and in his speech the main conditions for learning (for completing the learning process) aren't too hard to identify. So try to view the following as an expression of how a person analyzes a situation where the conditions for learning are poor.

"What I learned from not learning"

Harry: I've figured out what we're doing wrong as students and as instructors. Just stop for a second and try to remember how you felt when we got here last Monday. We were all a little tired from the trip, there were lots of new impressions, and a lot of faces we'd never seen before. Ralph was up there at the front, and we came in and obediently lined up for roll call.

Remember? All of us were deep in our own thoughts, and Ralph in his. He wasn't thinking about us; he was thinking about himself and what he planned to do next. We acted just like a theater audience, sitting there passively waiting for the actors to start the show.

Why did we do that? We did it because ever since we were in school, we've been trained to hand over all responsibility to the teacher. The person standing at the front is the person who decides.

Remember one day when we came in and there were compasses lying on our desks? All of a sudden we all started moving a little faster. And just as we were about to pick them up and look at them, he started yelling: "Don't touch the compasses! I said don't touch the compasses! They're not toys. They're extremely fine precision instruments."

It's enough to make you just give up and tune out. Then you don't learn anything. That's what I found out the first day. Obviously you have to have a chance to examine things yourself, to see how they work. That's when you start to think about things and ask questions, and that's when you get the motivation to learn. But to do that you have to be given the information you need—and no other. Here's what I mean:

Imagine you don't know me. We've never seen each other before. You're out in the lobby, talking to friends over a cup of coffee, and all of a sudden I come in. Remember, you've never seen me before. And I say: "To get to the men's washroom, go down one floor and then to the mezzanine below it. Then turn left, left again, and keep going down the hall and then turn right. Then you'll find the men's washroom on the left." And I walk out. You stand there scratching your head, wondering what that was all about.

But, then, say two hours later, you need to use the washroom. You start looking for the men's washroom and then you spot me. You come up to me, squirming and hopping from one foot to the other, and you say: "Listen, where was that washroom you were talking about?" And I say: "The washroom? Listen, did you know that even the ancient Greeks had special washrooms for men? They handed this custom down to the Romans, who improved the design of men's washrooms." You'd have had an accident long before I got to the Middle Ages!

And that's what most instructors do.

They either tell us things we don't need to know, or when we do need to know them, they tell us about something else. And what do we do about it? Nothing. We just suffer in silence, complacently listening.

So maybe we should take some of the blame. We sit there like sheep, with our heads propped up on our hands and with an eraser under an elbow to keep it from sliding, all of us skilled at unconsciously knowing when it's time to execute a knowledgeable nod. What's interesting about these nods is that it doesn't make any difference what the instructor said, whether it was a positive or negative statement, because with our nods we always seem to indicate that we agree.

So the instructor thinks we're all keeping up with him and drawing the same conclusions as he is. Well, we aren't. We sit there and let our bodies lie for us. We should all have litmus paper on our foreheads that shows whether we're keeping up or not, by turning green when we are and red when we get lost.

Basically, all of this boils down to the methods we use when we teach or learn.

I thought about that the other day. Have you ever watched a little kid learning to ride a bike? Now, can you imagine teaching your kids to ride a bike by giving them a lecture about it? I doubt it.

Let me try a little mental experiment on you. Assume that you don't know how to ride a bike, but you'd like to learn, so you sign up for a bike-riding course with me as your instructor. You're excited. You've often seen other people whiz by on their bikes, and it really looks like fun. And now you're finally going to learn to do the same thing.

The big day has arrived, and you're sitting there in the classroom. After a long introductory discussion about schedules, coffee breaks, and so on, it's finally time to get down to business. "First you have to learn the basics," I say, and then I take a picture of a bike and put it on the overhead projector. It contains the names of all of the parts of a bicycle in tiny print. To the people sitting way in the back, I say: "Sorry you can't see this, but you'll get a copy after the class." Those in the back nod gratefully and again slump back in their chairs.

As I said, first you have to learn the basics, so I run through the names of all of the bike parts, one after another after another. Then, when I get to the gears, I just can't restrain myself. I'm really interested in bike gears, so I go up to the flipchart and offer an 18-minute mini-lecture on how a 10-speed bike works. Then, I finish by saying: "But actually, that doesn't have anything to do with it."

Forty-eight minutes have gone by. There's no air left in the room. Your dream of learning to ride a bike has long since faded into oblivion. Your back hurts and your backside is numb. You're starting to doze off. Suddenly I say, "Now I'm going to explain how to ride a bike." You lean forward in expectation. Finally, you think. Then I say, "And riding a bike isn't as hard as it looks." Teachers always say that. They have a tendency to try to make us think things aren't what they are: "This isn't boring; you only think it is."

"Now as I said, riding a bike isn't as hard as it looks. You just stand on the left side of the bicycle with your hands on the handlebars. You place your left foot on the left pedal, which must be positioned at its lowest point. Your right foot should be on the ground, just behind your left foot. You push off with your right foot to give yourself and your bicycle some momentum. At this point, you'll have a tendency to fall. This tendency may be to the right or to the left. If it's to the right, turn the handlebars to the right while shifting your body's center of gravity to the left, and turn the handlebars back to the left. Once you and your bicycle have attained a steady forward momentum, move your right leg in a circular, counter-clockwise motion to the rear. This will bring you up into a sitting position on the seat. Then apply pressure to the pedal that is furthest forward while maintaining your balance as I indicated previously.

"Is that clear?" The listeners reply:

- "Yes."
- "Why?"
- "Because we already know how to ride a bike."

Exactly. You already know how to ride a bike. In fact, 80 percent of all instruction seems to have been developed for people who already know whatever it is they're supposed to be learning.

That's what I've just realized. If I'm going to learn anything, I'm going to have to draw my own conclusions based on my own experiences. I have to be involved, really involved.

That way I don't have to feel stupid, incompetent, and incapable. Instead I can feel intelligent, clever, and capable. That's what I learned from not learning this week.

And that's not too bad.*

---

*This speech was taken from the film "What I learned from not learning."

The student's plea

The thank-you speech (or whatever you want to call it) can be interpreted as a personal view of "how I'd like things to be." This is the speaker's/student's plea. (The parallel to the learning process is obvious.)

1. Don't stifle my natural curiosity, awaken it! In other words, don't take the "compass" away from me. Let me take part from the beginning, and create my own idea of why I should get involved in this course.

2. Just give me the information I need, not a bunch of information I don't need. In other words, I respect your knowledge, and I thank you for wanting to share it with me, but remember that the only reason you've been appointed to be my instructor is to give me the information that I need—the information that's meaningful to me.

3. Let me think things through myself and draw my own conclusions. In other words, don't abandon me, don't deny me my own path to conclusions and insight. Hold your enthusiasm and your impatience in check. Don't believe that your own conclusions based on your many years of experience, can be mine just because you tell me what they are.

4. Help me find words for the things I've understood! In other words, when you see that I understand, that I'm feeling it in my bones and saying "Aha!," help me find words and expressions for the things I've understood, so I can turn my insights into knowledge that I can handle.

5. Help me use my knowledge, so it doesn't wither away and become useless. In other words, give me a chance to test and expand and reinforce my knowledge. Show me how I can use it, so I can continue to learn on my own, aided by new experiences.

People want to learn

In his book *Moments of Truth*, Scandinavian Airlines President Jan Carlzon describes his view of the individual in the company: "We must now learn to see the New Person as a great opportunity, a resource still lacking in many parts of the world. The New Person is confident, well-educated and largely liberated from acute financial problems. This makes him ready to take on more qualified and responsible work."

Carlzon's observations are confirmed by surveys carried out at a number of companies. Bo Ekman, head of the Swedish Institute for Opinion Research, has this to say:

"Surveys of the attitudes of tens of thousands of employees with regard to commitment, loyalty, leadership, and efficiency reveal some important facts:

- People want to make a greater commitment at work.
- People strive for efficiency, and they have their own ideas about how work can be better organized.
- People want the kind of leadership and organization that allows them to make better use of their intellectual, emotional, and physical capabilities.
- People consistently feel that their loyalty to the company is greater than the loyalty and concern they receive in return.
- People want more training.
- People want to feel respected as human beings."

At many work places, the potential for increasing efficiency is enormous. A widespread problem is that the values upon which the work structure is based often differ completely from those of employees.

It seems that the people in the boardroom have discovered the individual. No one can deny that the New Person is making significant demands—and with good reason. As a result, the concept of leadership is also changing. The most important trend is that leadership seems to be evolving from "what the boss does" to a more or less unspoken mutual commitment between supervisors and their subordinates. Here we're talking about 200 percent responsibility—100 percent for the supervisor and 100 percent for the worker. (It's tempting to compare this new form of leadership with love: basically, love requires that both parties agree that they're in love!) So, at times it can seem absurd for "the boss to take a leadership course." It would be reasonable to assume that leadership develops best among the people involved. (What would be the sense of sending one-half of a loving couple to a course on loving?)

This basic view of leadership is gradually making its mark in the area of education. More and more, responsibility is being shared, and this sharing of responsibility is resulting in new forms of instruction whose objectives, content, and methods are compatible with the individual's own knowledge and spontaneous learning process. As a result, classroom instruction is no longer considered the universal method for meeting learning needs that it once was. (This approach was typical of the "specialist view" that used to prevail in companies. Or, as Mark Twain put it, "To those who only have a hammer as a tool, all problems tend to look like nails.")

People today are looking for other solutions. Participation in projects, on-the-job training in other departments, etc., have become increasingly common. But there are also signs that training is moving from the classroom to the conference room, which means that department and group supervisors are becoming the instructors of the people working under them— precisely what they as supervisors are supposed to be.

That's why training materials are being developed that are specifically designed for such use. The benefits are obvious: travel time and absence from work are eliminated; the group can concentrate on the things that are directly related to its own operations; training can be scheduled in accordance with the work load; "joint learning" makes it easier to use the knowledge acquired; each individual's own experiences and prior knowledge can better be shared with the other members of the group, leadership can be developed through mutual knowledge of each participant's expertise and interests, and so on and so forth.

There are some other major trends. Increasingly, the choice and formulation of course objectives is being based on what the learner feels he or she needs to do a certain job better. In the past, course objectives often amounted to a formal list of items of knowledge that the student was required to elucidate at the end of the course. ("What is a Panhard rod?" "What is the formula for calculating return on investment?") The second question concentrates on rote memorization, while the first stresses genuine understanding.

The emphasis has gone from "teaching about a phenomenon" to "teaching how to do something." We don't take a course to "learn abut marketing." Our purpose is to learn "how to market."

More and more, course content is being designed to provide a framework for the learner's process of experimentation and discovery, rather than, as in the past, to turn students into walking reference books or champions of total recall.

As students become increasingly active and involved, the climate in which a lecturer on high merely engages in "sausage-stuffing" tends to disappear.

In his book *Experiential Learning*, Kolb defines learning in the same way: "Learning is the process whereby knowledge is created through the transformation of experience."

Thus, the main task of education is to take learners' earlier experiences and use them to give the learners opportunities to acquire new ones.

Students are on their way to being treated as adults.

Congratulations!

3.
Sources of inspiration

What is it that makes
a film or text "good?"
What is it that makes a speaker
convincing?
What is it, really, that gets us
involved, that captures
our attention
and that allows us to learn?

Influences

Sometimes I wonder why education has isolated itself in its own private world for so long. Advances and improvements in teaching methods have been practically nonexistent, while the breakthroughs achieved in other forms of communication have been enormous. I don't mean technological breakthroughs; I'm talking about new and better ways to adapt these forms of communication to the human brain.

I've already implied that disciplines other than education and psychology are being used today as sources of inspiration—by teachers seeking models for planning lessons, and by students that want to learn more about their individual ways of reacting to different "communications methods."

One such discipline, which is closely related to education, is classical rhetoric. Rhetoric (the art of speaking) has for thousands of years been an essential subject of study for everyone (not the least of whom are politicians) with an ambition to teach and influence other people. And market forces have continually refined this discipline by providing an immediate indication of its effects: no skillful rhetoric, no influence, and no power.

What we call dramatic arts, an important discipline for filmmaking, is similarly being polished by market forces: no "good film," no public, and no box-office success. Of course, this also applies to the theater and other forms of literature.

The same is true in advertising: no effective ads, no sales, and no more commissions for the admen.

What skills do all of these experts possess? What are their secrets? What makes them successful? And even though we're talking mostly about "one-way communications," the techniques work. Why?

A question immediately arises: is it ethical to resort to theatrical tricks to manipulate people this way, to make them believe things they don't want to believe? Is it right to use dramatic techniques to get people to adopt one political viewpoint rather than another? Is it right to use clever marketing and sales techniques to induce people to buy a certain product?

Perhaps by considering the exact opposite we can arrive at a more important conclusion. By understanding how other people try to influence us and by understanding how we react, we can develop greater self-confidence and more analytical ways of thinking that open the door to richer learning.

If these disciplines really have so much influence over the rest of society, why haven't they had any effect on ordinary education until quite recently?

Can it possibly be, as I've already discussed, that the school—the good old-fashioned school with stern old-maid schoolteachers, awe-inspiring principals, desks and pupils all lined up in a row—still serves, albeit unconsciously, as our strongest model? Is it our reminiscences of our own school years that force us into the traditional roles of student and teacher? Is this why our behavior is different when we attend a course (a formal education setting) than it would otherwise be—an unconscious imitation of our conceptions (memories) of how students and teachers are supposed to behave?

I don't know. Many people think so, but others feel that this is an exaggerated and unnecessarily pessimistic description of the school as an institution, and that we should instead seek an explanation in companies' and especially, management's values.

Some believe that the way people behave in a course setting is a direct reflection, practically a caricature, of the company's culture—an indication of how these people perceive the relationship between supervisors and subordinates.

But regardless of what the (unconscious) models were in the past, people are increasingly seeking other models and sources of inspiration, for instance, from the disciplines of rhetoric and drama. What is it that makes a film or text "good"? What is it that makes a speaker convincing? What is it, really, that gets us involved, that captures our attention, and allows us to learn?

Drama

D rama is usually described as the art of telling a story. This ability is what makes authors and filmmakers successful. But how do they do it?

Ola Olson, a respected Swedish dramatist, has made some valuable reflections on this. They're presented here more or less as I remember them. Suppose you're watching the beginning of a film. In it, a man is walking down the street. The narrator says "This is Joe Doakes. He's 33 years old and works at a large company, where his job is to . . ."

Sounds dull, doesn't it? And it doesn't look as though the rest of the film will be any better. As a dramatist, Ola proposes a different introduction.

The film starts with a close-up of empty beer cans floating around in a bathtub. The camera pulls back, revealing more beer cans. A pair of wet hands opens yet another can. Close-up of a wet foot getting out of the bathtub. A towel wraps around a body. Steps. The refrigerator door opens. More beer. The whole bathtub is full of floating beer cans. The man climbs back into the tub.

You wonder "Who the hell is this guy?" And just then the narrator says "This is Joe Doakes. He's 33 years old and works at a large company, where his job is to . . ."

This is precisely the same method that a child uses when he or she says "Guess which hand it's in?" The difference is that Ola Olson consciously planned to elicit a certain reaction from us, while the child does it spontaneously.

How do western films usually start? In any case, they don't start with somebody saying "Welcome to this film. It is about good and evil. At the conclusion of this film you will have learned that good triumphs over evil" (happy ending), or "that evil triumphs over good" (tragic ending). Instead, we see a shootout, a bank robbery or some other dramatic event.

Or we might see something more low-key, in a more "artistic" cinematic style. The film starts with a shot of steps leading into a saloon. The heat is overpowering. A kitten licks its fur. The saloon doors fly open. We see the legs of a man dressed in dark clothes. A kick. A shrill howl from the kitten. The legs move off to the right. Silence. A pair of legs dressed in white come up the stairs. The man bends down and pets the cat tenderly, and moves off-camera to the left. This is more than enough to tell us what the film is about: the struggle between good (in white clothes) and evil (in dark clothes), personified by two men. "What's going to happen?"

In the jargon of the dramatic arts, the introduction to a film is called the opening. The opening is designed not only to get us generally interested or excited; its primary goal is to establish the film's main conflict. (Next time you see a film, try to note what opening the filmmaker used, and how it was structured.)

Milos Forman is one of today's most skillful filmmakers. The opening of his highly acclaimed film *One Flew Over the Cuckoo's Nest* is already considered a classic. He uses a number of devices—details that are hard to discern as individual entities, but which affect the whole and our perception of events—to present the two main characters (antagonists).

Forman even uses the same camera angle in the first scene in which Nurse Ratched (Louise Fletcher) arrives at the mental hospital, as he does in the scene where McMurphy (Jack Nicholson) arrives. (Because these introductory scenes are so entrancing, you'll have to look at them several times before you can see the "mechanics" behind them.)

So the function of the opening is to create an exciting situation and expectation. But what happens then? (See illustrations on page 86.)

After the opening (attention) stage, we come to the exposition of crisis (information) stage, where the viewers are supposed to learn who's who, what their relationships are, what the scene of the action looks like, and so on. This is often the most boring part of a film, and it's not always easy to keep track of things.

Here the skills of the author are really put to the test. He or she has to give us only necessary but sufficient information in a way that makes it interesting. (In less successful films, the lines of the actors can be comically artificial in order to give the viewer information. "Only you can help us, Flash. Emperor Ming, evil ruler of the Galactic Empire, is planning to attack Earth!")

This is followed by the escalation of conflict stage.

NURSE RATCHED: Severe coiffure—Waves key ring around (power).—Rigid posture and pounding gait (alone).—Steel door (slams).—Red lamp lights up.—Polished floor.—Hard, cold lighting (synthetic interior).

McMURPHY: Cap.—Whistles (coming from freedom).—Casual clothes.—Dances (the hero's arrival).—Contact with peers (the patients).—Soft, warm lighting (serene classical music).

Let me say here that all drama is based on conflicts and tensions between opposing forces: good and evil in different guises, or the known and the unknown. In the escalation of conflict stage, the struggle is depicted in a way that prompts the viewer to ask "What's going to happen?" The plot moves forward toward the climax.

The climax, or conflict resolution, ends the struggle. Here we find out who the murderer was. Either the hero or the villain emerges victorious from the last duel. The car chase ends with a crash. The sinister plot is revealed. Everything is explained.

In the fade-out, we see the main character "ride off into the sunset," one experience richer. We also leave the movie theater one experience richer, and with no important questions left unanswered (unless the filmmaker's intention was precisely to leave us with questions unanswered).

This narrative pattern, these five main elements, don't apply only to the film as a whole; each large sequence (gestalt) in the film and, often, even individual scenes, are presented following the same pattern.

And this technique works, for the simple reason that that's the way our minds work (the learning process).

To illustrate this dimension of the dramatic arts, we've taken another film classic, *High Noon*, and cut it into small pieces, to give you a chance to play the role of author. You don't have to have seen the film to do this exercise.

On pages 89–90, we describe 15 scenes from the film in random order. Try to arrange them in the order that corresponds to the narrative method of drama.

The correct solution (how the scenes are actually arranged in the film) is given on pages 91–92.

A. While Will and the gang leader face each other on the town's main street, the members of the gang take up sniper positions on rooftops around the town. It's just after 12 ("High Noon").

B. The leader of the gang arrives at the train station, where he's met by three gang members.

C. The townspeople emerge cheering from their hiding places.

D. Will and Amy get married at the sheriff's office. Will puts his gun and badge away for good. Now they intend to settle in the country.

E. A shot. The gang leader falls to the ground, dead.

F. Under a tree on a hilltop outside a town, three swarthy riders meet. They ride into town and sit down at the railroad station. It is a quarter to eleven in the morning.

G. Will and Amy leave town, but out on the prairie Will decides to turn back and meet his destiny.

H. A telegraph messenger rushes in to say that the gang leader has been released from jail and that he's on his way to town to kill the sheriff who put him there.

I. The couple leaves town for a new life elsewhere.

J. Problem: Will has promised Amy that he will never resort to violence again. She threatens to divorce him if he stays. The terrified townspeople let him down and don't dare help him.

K. Amy realizes how brave her husband is, and her growing sense of admiration convinces her to return to town, and even to pick up a gun and shoot the gang leader.

L. Amy and Will get back in their buggy. And as we said: when danger gets close enough, even Quakers must take up arms.

M. Will's determination is presented. He wants to stay and deal with the problem, to fight it out with the gang leader.

N. Will arrives alone at the empty town, where he meets the gang leader. They decide to have a showdown.

O. Will stands in light-colored clothes at one end of the street. The dark-clad gang leader stands at the other end.

Opening	**Exposition**	**Escalation**	**Resolution**	**Fade-out**
SCENES:	SCENES:	SCENES:	SCENES	SCENES:

—— —— ——   —— —— ——   —— —— ——   —— —— ——

How would you tell this story? See the next page for the right answer.

Here is the order of the scenes in the film. The main conflict is presented in the first scene (opening). By starting with the "three nasty-looking riders," the director transmits to the viewer a feeling of danger—but danger from what?

The romance of the wedding provides contrast. We don't find out what the danger is until the telegraph messenger arrives. In the next section, the director presents the hero's inner conflict. Here we receive necessary and sufficient information about Will's hard choice, before the drama escalates.

"What's going to happen?"

Opening

F. Under a tree on a hilltop outside a town, three swarthy riders meet. They ride into town and sit down at the railroad station. It is a quarter to eleven in the morning.

D. Will and Amy get married at the sheriff's office. Will puts his gun and badge away for good. Now they intend to settle in the country.

H. A telegraph messenger rushes in to say that the gang leader has been released from jail and that he's on his way to town to kill the sheriff who put him there.

Exposition

M. Will's determination is presented. He wants to stay and deal with the problem, to fight it out with the gang leader.

J. Problem: Will has promised Amy that he will never resort to violence again. She threatens to divorce him if he stays. The terrified townspeople let him down and don't dare help him.

G. Will and Amy leave town, but out on the prairie Will decides to turn back and meet his destiny.

Escalation of conflict

B. The leader of the gang arrives at the train station, where he's met by three gang members.

N. Will arrives alone at the empty town, where he meets the gang leader. They decide to have a show-down.

A. While Will and the gang leader face each other on the town's main street, the members of the gang take up sniper positions on rooftops around the town. It's just after 12 noon ("High Noon").

Conflict resolution

O. Will stands in light-colored clothes at one end of the street. The dark-clad gang leader stands at the other end.

E. A shot. The gang leader falls to the ground, dead.

K. Amy realizes how brave her husband is, and her growing sense of admiration con-vinces her to return to town, and even to pick up a gun and shoot the gang leader.

Fade-out

C.   The   townspeople emerge cheering from their hiding places.

L. Amy and Will get back in their buggy. And as we said: when danger gets close enough, even Quakers must take up arms.

I.   The   couple   leaves town   for   a   new   life elsewhere.

THE LEARNING PROCESS	DRAMA
Interest, curiosity Mental preparedness and receptiveness.	**Opening** Establish the film's main conflict – Good vs evil – The known vs the unknown.
Information Facts and data are converted into information.	**Exposition of crisis** Who's who? What's the problem? What are the relative strengths of the characters?
Processing Information is converted into experience and insight.	**Escalation of conflict** The duel: "What's going to happen?"
Conclusion Experience and insight are converted into knowledge.	**Conflict resolution** The climax "So that's what happened..."
Application Knowledge is converted into skills and attitudes – and wisdom.	**Fade-out** One experience richer.

The learning process (how we learn spontaneously) and the main principles of drama (the art of telling a story) are astonishingly similar.

When we (Ola Olson, Krister Nathanaelson, and I) created this exercise, I learned something interesting: It's been said that the film was ordered by the Central Intelligence Agency (CIA) to win the support of the American people for the war in Korea. The message, the premise of the film, is presented vividly as a conclusion, in the scene where we discover that it was Will's wife who shot the gang leader. In other words: When danger (communism) threatens, even the most peace-loving Quaker (the American people) must take up arms.

And in that sense it works, of course, because we're overjoyed when Will's wife shoots the villain. She becomes our heroine, just as stipulated in the blueprints.

Rhetoric

It's probably correct to say that the dramatic arts have their roots in classical rhetoric. I asked Kurt Johannesson, Sweden's only professor of rhetoric, to briefly describe the elements of rhetoric. Here's what he says:

Rhetoric is the art of speaking, that is, the art of talking or writing in a way that makes people listen and understand—and be persuaded. Long ago, the ancient Greeks noted that convincing speeches and texts were usually constructed the same way. In other words, there are some simple rules that we can easily remember and try to use to make our language more effective.

Let's say that we're trying to sell the premise, message, or thesis, that "men and women should have equal rights and opportunities." But who are our listeners? How are they likely to react if we present such a thesis? Let's imagine that they come from a fairly large, modern company. If so, we have to have an introduction that awakens interest in, empathy for, and confidence in the speaker. Otherwise, people will instantly decide not to listen. In rhetoric, this introduction is called the exordium. Here's an example:

We can all see the enormous changes taking place in our society, and I believe that these changes are going to influence the business world and our company. We're going to be faced with problems that will have to be solved if we are to survive and grow. But I also believe that the future holds great promise if we do the right things.

Now people are listening; this is important. Then we sketch the background to what we're talking about—only in general terms, and we refer only to things that people are aware of and immediately accept as fact. In rhetoric, this is called the *narratio*, which, as you may have guessed, means narration. For an example:

In earlier times, men and women did completely different things—at home and in the community. "Adam plowed and Eve spun" as they used to say, or, as we learned in our first-grade readers, Dad fixes the screen door and Mom bakes pies. But now these differences are being wiped out everywhere. Look at sports: women are playing soccer and running in marathons. Look at fashions: men and women both wear jeans, but fortunately, the shapes are a little different.

In this way the speaker creates a rapport—a "we" feeling with the listeners.

And only now do we come to the premise, or thesis, because we know that a lot of people don't like this idea or are unsure. That's why we're giving this speech, to convince them, to overcome their resistance. This is called the *propositio*, which needs no translation. Example:

The time has come for us to strive to provide equal opportunities for men and women in our company (or industry) as well.

And now we have to present arguments quickly to support this proposal or demand, but not too many—three at the most, and only those that can convince precisely this audience. For example:

'There are no longer any heavy jobs that women can't do. There may have been such jobs in the past, but now we have machines to help us. It would be a waste if our company didn't make use of

women's talents and ambition. They will surely be needed in the
future, when good people will be even harder to find. Moreover, all
modern management research and experience shows that "male"
and "female" characteristics must complement each other—even in
the highest positions and in the most crucial decision making.

And after this *argumentatio*, it's time for the conclusion, or
peroratio. There the speaker summarizes briefly, very briefly,
the most important things he or she has said, to imprint them
firmly in people's memory. Then the speaker tries to arouse
their enthusiasm and determination with a closing appeal
where the main ingredients are fervor and emotion, like this:

> So we have to start working now to make this happen. I believe
> that such a policy represents an enormous opportunity for us to
> prevail in the battle with our competitors, and to meet the
> demands of the future.

When Franklin D. Roosevelt was elected president of the
United States in 1932, the country was in the grip of a brutal
depression. Innumerable companies were wiped out and many
millions of people were unemployed. In his inaugural address,
Roosevelt tried to persuade Americans that his New Deal, a
totally new economic and social policy, was absolutely necessary. Here are a few paragraphs from his famous speech. They
correspond to the five parts that, according to the rules of
rhetoric, a good speech should have: exordium, narratio, propositio, argumentatio, and peroratio.

But here we've changed the order of these five paragraphs.
How do you think they were arranged in Roosevelt's speech?

(A) We face the arduous days that lie before us in the warm
courage of the nation's unity: with the clean satisfaction that comes
from the stern performance of duty by old and young alike.

(B) I am certain that my fellow Americans expect that on my
induction into the presidency I will address them with a candor
and a decision which the present situation of our nation impels.
This is preeminently the time to speak the truth, the whole truth,
frankly, and boldly.

(C) This nation asks for action, and action now. This is no
unsolvable problem if we face it wisely and courageously . . . treat-
ing the task as we would treat the emergency of war.

(D) The withered leaves of industrial enterprise lie on every side: farmers find no markets for their produce; the savings of many years in thousands of families are gone. More important, a host of unemployed citizens face the grim problem of existence.

(E) There must be a strict supervision of all banking and credits and investments, there must be an end to speculation with other people's money, and there must be provision for an adequate but sound currency.

SUGGESTED ORDER: _____
Correct order on page 99.

Advertising

We can find another parallel in advertising. According to the traditional criteria, a good ad has to meet precisely the same requirements:

1. Attention (illustration and/or heading)
2. Information (about the offer)
3. A challenge to the reader (compare it to the alternatives)
4. A conclusion ("Ours is better, isn't it?")
5. A call to action ("Send in the coupon or call.")

There is yet another interesting parallel in the way we view customers in connection with marketing. And I'm not talking only about advertising (see above). In marketing, especially of capital goods (both to companies and private individuals), we assume that the customer goes through a number of stages (learning) before deciding what to buy.

The highly respected marketing expert Philip Kotler describes this as a stepwise elimination of alternatives. When a need arises (for a new car, for instance), there are many alternatives—all of the car models the person knows about, although his or her interest in information will be limited to only a few of these models. Customers make their choices spontaneously, in accordance with their needs, their interests, and their pocketbooks. Finally, there are perhaps only a few alternatives left, and in many cases the differences that determine the final choice are extremely small. The role of marketing can thus be likened to that of a teacher: to support, step by step, this process in a way that leads to the conclusion that the marketer/teacher wants the customer/learner to draw.

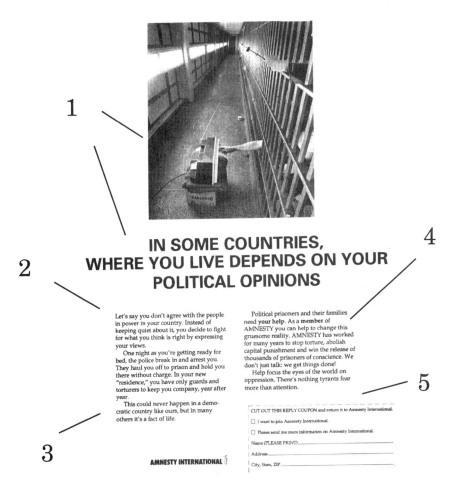

1

2

3

4

5

IN SOME COUNTRIES, WHERE YOU LIVE DEPENDS ON YOUR POLITICAL OPINIONS

Let's say you don't agree with the people in power in your country. Instead of keeping quiet about it, you decide to fight for what you think is right by expressing your views.

One night as you're getting ready for bed, the police break in and arrest you. They haul you off to prison and hold you there without charge. In your new "residence," you have only guards and torturers to keep you company, year after year.

This could never happen in a democratic country like ours, but in many others it's a fact of life.

Political prisoners and their families need **your help**. As a **member** of AMNESTY you can help to change this gruesome reality. AMNESTY has worked for many years to stop torture, abolish capital punishment and win the release of thousands of prisoners of conscience. We don't just talk: we get things done!

Help focus the eyes of the world on oppression. There's nothing tyrants fear more than attention.

AMNESTY INTERNATIONAL

> CUT OUT THIS REPLY COUPON and return it to Amnesty International.
> ☐ I want to join Amnesty International.
> ☐ Please send me more information on Amnesty International.
> Name (PLEASE PRINT)
> Address
> City, State, ZIP

A good ad has to satisfy the conditions for learning.

THE LEARNING PROCESS
Interest, curiosity
Mental preparedness and
receptiveness.

DECISION TO BUY
Awareness
We become aware of
a need to start to
look at alternatives.

Information
Facts and data are converted
into information.

Receptiveness
We're receptive to
information about
some of these
alternatives.

Processing
Information is converted
into experience and insight.

Comparison
We compare the
alternatives,
consciously and
unconsciously.

Conclusion
Experience and insight are
converted into knowledge.

Decision
We make up our
mind and close the
deal.

Application
Knowledge is converted into
skills and attitudes—and
wisdom.

Experience
Our experience will
determine whether
we're satisfied and
whether we'll come
back next time.

Philip Kotler describes this version of the learning process as a step-wise elimination of alternatives.

This series of pictures offers one description of these stages. First, an impulse, or interest, makes the customer receptive to information on different alternatives, which in turn leads to a comparison (processing) of this information, which leads to a conclusion, which leads to action: the purchase.

We determine what marketing, media, and messages to use on the basis of where in this process we think the prospect is.

So we find the same pattern again and again: the politician who persuades, the salesman who convinces, the author who engrosses, the preacher who preaches, the opponent who advocates, and the teacher who teaches. Even in research, where knowledge is created, the pattern is the same.

- A thought, or hypothesis, serves as the starting point.
- Data (information) is collected.
- The information is processed and studied.
- A conclusion is drawn. ("The hypothesis was right/wrong.")
- The results are used.

So, why shouldn't we use the same method when we plan formal teaching and learning activities? Why shouldn't we try to transmit knowledge using the same methods that were used when that knowledge came into being? In the words of Piaget, "To understand is to invent."

Correct order of Roosevelt's speech (pages 95–96): B, D, C, E, A.

4.
Short cuts

**Half as much,
twice as good.**

Putting learning on fast-forward

H alf as much, twice as good: is it possible? The media explosion has changed our way of looking at information. Umberto Eco defines information like this: "an uncontrollable number of messages that each of us can mix together in his or her own way by pushing buttons on the remote control." We're living in the age of fast-forward and channel-changing. Anyone who happens to write about the right thing in the right way at the right time has a good chance of being elevated to the status of guru, and his or her book must be read before the next guru takes over. Books have become perishable items. The offering of newspapers, magazines, and trade journals is so huge that a large part of what is purchased is not read, or is just subjected to a fairly disorganized speed-reading. The risk of drowning in information is real and imminent. Eco says, "The consumer may not be any freer than he was before, but the ways of teaching him to be free and in control are undoubtedly changing."

This is basically a matter of our goals for our own learning: if we want to avoid falling victim to other people's knowledge, we have to try to master our own.

With the right attitudes and the right tools, we can do that. When we do, we'll be able to pick and choose (change channels and fast-forward) consciously, systematically, and with a specific goal in mind. We'll be able to extract everything worth extracting from a technical book in a fraction of the time it would take to read it. The contents of product manuals and other internal information can be cut to one-half, one-third, or less. And we'll be ready to make training more efficient by applying the concept of "half as much, twice as good."

Anyone who happens to write about the right thing in the right way at the right time has a good chance of being elevated to the status of guru, and his or her book must be read before the next guru takes over.

You don't have to be a politician, journalist, or adman to apply the basic principles of drama and rhetoric. These principles are also an excellent tool for teaching—ourselves as well as others. But how we apply the principles depends on what role we happen to be playing. I've decided to discuss each case separately:

1. When we're pure "transmitters" (writing a lecture, an article, or a lesson plan)
2. When we participate in a course and share responsibility with the instructor
3. When we're pure "receivers" (reading a book or being "subjected" to instruction)

The premise is that, regardless of which one of these situations we find ourselves in, we can be much more effective if we make use of our prior knowledge of our own learning process and the tools in the experts' tool boxes. The following sections present a number of practical recommendations about how we can do this. Some of them are easy to apply, while others are more ambitious. Here are the main points covered in each section:

The Big Picture First

Here I describe the importance of creating an early overview of a subject's main features, especially in cases where the frames of reference of the instructor and the learners are different.

Being Pedagogical

Let's say you write a text of some kind—an article, a report, an investment proposal, a lecture, or a speech. Such a text can always be made more accessible and more worth reading through pedagogical editing. (Films are edited this way; the editor selects the various scenes and decides how to arrange them.) The author reviews the presentation's construction in general to determine the order in which the various parts should be introduced. As this is done, the author usually switches sections of the text around, cuts the material down, and makes a few small additions.

In basically the same way, you can carry out a pedagogical revision (checking) when you want to study the work of others—texts, video films, lesson plans, or course packages—to evaluate their pedagogical effectiveness.

Mindmapping

Mindmapping is a note-taking technique that coincides better than traditional techniques with the way we associate. Try it yourself.

Mindmapping has become an invaluable tool for many people involved in creative work, problem solving, and training.

Collaborative Learning

If we as instructors and learners are to share responsibility, then there are a number of things we have to do. Evaluating the foregoing session isn't enough; it's even more important for all of us together to try to decide how the coming session should be arranged, which doesn't mean that the preparations made up to that point have to be thrown out. This chapter offers examples of things we can do.

The Art of Studying

Can you read a thick technical book in a couple of hours? Not if you want to remember any of it. But if I ask, "Can you get everything of value out of a thick technical book in a couple of hours?" then the answer is yes. In this chapter, I present the learning method that people accustomed to studying and reading use—most often spontaneously.

The fact is that if the author hasn't done any pedagogical editing, you can do it yourself when you read a book, using your own learning process as a base.

Other Ways

Quite often, formal education isn't the best way to solve a learning problem. Here I give some examples of alternatives.

Seeing the big picture first

W hat's the shortest distance between two points? How may sides does a sheet of paper have? These are simple questions with given answers: the shortest distance between two points is a straight line; a sheet of paper has two sides: a front side and a back side. These statements are obviously true, or are they?

Now suppose you're going to teach these "truths" to an ant that has lived all of its life on the surface of a balloon. For the ant, the statement that the shortest distance between two points is a straight line isn't true; the shortest distance is a curved line. Or what if the ant lived instead on a Möbius strip? Then the statement that a sheet of paper has two sides wouldn't be valid; a sheet of paper would have only one side.

Everyone who tries to study and understand Einstein's theory of relativity or the principles of quantum mechanics runs into the same problem as the ant in the example. Things wouldn't be any better if the ant tried to teach you. "As you already know, dear student, the shortest distance between two points is a curved line. This is an axiom, that is, a truth that cannot be questioned." Since this statement completely contradicts your earlier experiences (and knowledge) your possibilities of learning anything from this ant-teacher are slim, to say the least.

The difference between the ant's frame of reference and your own make learning impossible—unless you're already familiar with and understand the ant's frame of reference. Suppose now that that was precisely what the ant was trying to do—to teach you to understand its world. Then we run into a logical blind alley. In order to make any sense out of this instruction, you must already have the knowledge of where the instruction is supposed to lead (A situation that occurs far too often in real life).

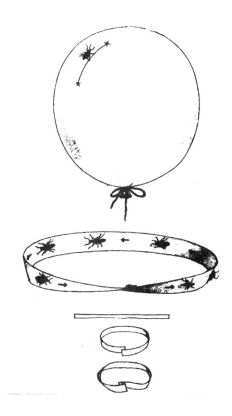

"As you already know, dear student, the shortest distance between two points is a curved line. This is an axiom, that is, a truth that cannot be questioned." "A sheet of paper has only one side, a front side." (Try it yourself. Cut a strip of paper and glue the ends together as shown in the figure. Follow the ant's path along the strip with your finger and you'll see that the strip has only one side!)

If the ant had been a good and wise teacher, it would have invited you to spend some time on the balloon to give you a chance to discover this new world for yourself. Then it would have been much easier for you to understand what the ant was telling you because you could use your new experiences as a starting point.

This method is obviously the best method for learning, say, motor skills, such as riding a bike: we experiment, with or without help, and we discover, step by step, at our own pace and on our own terms, what we should do. This is an example of learning by doing.

The point I'm making is that this teaching method should just as obviously be considered the best method for all learning—even learning involving abstract knowledge. To show concretely what I mean, I'll transfer these ant and bicycle analogies to a typical university and company-training subject: business finance.

When people without much business experience start studying business finance, they can easily fall into a maze of theoretical lines of reasoning that make it extremely difficult for them to understand what all of these things really have to do with each other. (I've personally had this experience many times, both as a student in the traditional sense and as a teacher of this subject.) What these beginners need first of all is experience of their own that is related in some way to this subject's frame of reference. (Compare this with the ant-and-balloon analogy.) Secondly, they need a model of this frame of reference that they can use to test and discover different relationships for themselves. (Compare this with how we learn to ride a bike.)

I've have had the privilege of developing and introducing such a model—a physical simulation of the most important relationships in business finance ("LMI Apples & Oranges"): it shows how purchasing routines, competition, the choice of production equipment, and other influences affect a company's profitability. In this simulation, several groups of participants run "companies" in competition with each other. Each group (three to four people) can decide for itself what it's going to produce, how it's going to produce it, and so forth. But most importantly, the participants can see the consequences of their decisions—not in the form of a computer printout, but as easy-to-observe "movement" of their company's capital. Here's an example.

A company's balance sheet shows where in the company the capital is: cash, raw materials, and finished products. Thus, it serves as a snapshot of the company at a certain point in time—at the end of the year, for instance.

At the end of the following year, the new balance sheet will differ from the old one as a result of everything that happened during the year. These balance sheets don't tell a layman very much. Even if each line in a report is understandable in itself, it reveals nothing to the layman about the dynamics and the cause-and-effect relationships that prevailed during the period between the two snapshots. With a little exaggeration, we can say that this is like looking at a snapshot from the beginning of a film and one from the end of the same film, and then trying to

ASSETS			LIABILITIES AND EQUITY		
Current Assets	Year 1	Year 2	**Liabilities**	Year 1	Year 2
Cash	17	30	Taxes	1	3
Accounts receivable	12	9	Short-term loans	13	9
Raw materials and WIP	11	13	Long-term loans	7	11
Finished goods	8	4	**Total liabilities**	**21**	**23**
Total current assets	**48**	**56**	**Equity**		
Fixed assets			Share capital/stock	5	5
Real property	20	20	Retained earnings	48	50
Plant and equipment	8	5	Net profit for the year	2	3
Total fixed assets	**28**	**25**	**Total equity**	**55**	**58**
TOTAL ASSETS	**75**	**81**	TOTAL LIABILITIES/EQUITY	**76**	**81**

What can the uninitiated learn from these figures which show what happened to the company during the year?

decide whether the film was good or not.

In the simulation model, the participants start by placing money markers, which represent the company's capital, on a board that shows schematically the various departments of the company. Each of these departments corresponds basically to one line of the balance sheet. The result is a three-dimensional overview of the balance sheet, but it's still no more than a snapshot.

Then the participants make decisions involving purchasing, production, product development, sales, etc. Each such decision is followed by a movement of capital from one section of the board to another. For example, when a purchase is made, capital is moved from cash to inventory to illustrate that the material has been bought and paid for. (This is precisely the same principle used in accounting, where the capital in cash decreases and the capital in inventory increases by the same amount when material is purchased.)

The participants continue this way all "year," and all movements of capital can be observed step by step. At the end of the year, we have a new snapshot/balance sheet. In this way, the participants make the entire "film" themselves; their decisions determine the course of events and what the individual "scenes" will look like. Now the snapshots at the beginning and end (the balance sheets) make some sense, and the participants can see the connection between their actions and the outcome.

In short, they've learned something about the business dynamics of a company, which is essential if the training is going to mean anything to them. (To return one last time to our analogies, they've visited the ant on its balloon, and they've tried to ride a bike.)

But the simulation does more than this. By encouraging the participants to use their earlier knowledge and experiences, the simulation creates conditions in which the learners can learn more than they are taught. In other words, the learning content is greater than the teaching content. And that's the

The model can be used to simulate a company's operations—the circulation of capital. The markers symbolize money and value. The cups are "cost carriers" that represent a certain quantity of material, components, work in progress, or a finished product.

whole idea behind the new method of teaching and learning.

The objective of conventional teaching is to connect one element of knowledge to the next. We can liken this to trying to solve a jigsaw puzzle by starting in the upper left-hand corner and then putting all the pieces in place in the right order, from left to right and from top to bottom. (If most of the picture's background consists of blue sky, this can be a dreary task.) We can say that this traditional form of education is linear.

Even user instructions and directions, or computer programs, are often laid out this way, although we occasionally see signs of other approaches. The learner has few opportunities to make use of his or her own experiences, because without an overview there's no room for them.

The opportunities for gaining new experiences are also limited. The result is fragmented knowledge—knowledge that's both hard to access and hard to use. That is one of industry's main criticisms of university-level education. This linear, "bit-by-bit" instruction is often evaluated quantitatively. Knowledge is viewed as a quantity that can be measured, even though the qualitative aspects of knowledge are what determine how useful it is.

The new teaching method (or, rather, learning method) tries instead to create a bird's-eye view, a total gestalt that can then be studied and restudied from different perspectives and in different degrees of detail.

This form of teaching can be called organic, or system-oriented. The overview provides room for earlier experiences, as well as opportunities for gaining new ones.

Old and new "knowledge gestalts" can be fitted into the pattern and filled out. The number of associations than can be related to the whole, and thus, the quality of the knowledge increases dramatically. To return to the jigsaw puzzle analogy, this way of teaching and learning corresponds to a more feasible way of solving a puzzle. We do the edges (the frame of reference) first, then we assemble prominent gestalts, and so forth.

In one case, we were asked to train the representatives (salespeople) of an American pharmaceutical company. The training involved a new drug designed primarily to combat high blood pressure, and the objective was to help these people understand the differences between the functional properties of the company's drug and of the competitors' products. We soon found that the representatives were well-educated in general, but that they lacked an overview that would enable them to make any sense out of a comparison of the various products.

So instead of trying to tack additional fragments onto the fragmentary knowledge they already had, we decided to let the students "rediscover" the human circulatory system, with emphasis on the characteristics that would later make a com-

The participants worked in groups of four, where they "rediscovered" the human circulatory system, filled in the blank spots in their earlier fragmentary knowledge, and placed all of this in an overall view of the system. The exercise was designed to help the participants identify the various subsystems shown in the pictures, and to determine their functions and the relationships between them. (Reproduced with permission from Pfizer International, New York.)

parison of the company's and competitors' products meaningful.

We presented the circulatory system on a Work Mat™ (see the previous page) and invited the participants to identify the anatomical and physiological characteristics that together regulate the blood circulation and blood pressure of a healthy person. The participants worked in small groups, and the exercises they completed on the Work Mat™ helped them to discover the relationships.

The pace of learning was determined by each group's previous knowledge. This exercise led to an overall understanding of the whole, of the "big picture," that provided plenty of room for the participants' prior knowledge and experiences. Thus equipped, the participants then did an exercise that enabled them to investigate and find out where in the circulatory system the competing drugs work.

The entire course was arranged this way, and as a result, it took a little over a week (instead of the planned eight weeks) to complete the training, with greater retention, greater self-confidence, and higher sales.

Actually, the basic idea behind both of these solutions isn't especially original. What is perhaps surprising is that this form of instruction is based on self-evident principles that we apply spontaneously when we teach our children to ride a bike. (See Harry's absurd description in an earlier section.) It isn't hard to see that the "bicycle lecture" may lead to the participants' "knowing more" (remembering more words and expressions—at least for a short time), but learning of a more "hands-on" nature results in knowledge of a totally different kind. This is the difference between the quantitative and qualitative views of knowledge.

Moreover, both examples deal with known and well-established frames of reference (the "balance sheet" and "anatomy/physiology"), so there is no conflict between the learners' prior knowledge/experiences and the material being taught.

In cases where instruction is based on frames of reference or ideas other than those the learners bring with them, the need to create an overview at an early stage is even greater. We live in an age of model-swapping, or, to use a currently fashionable

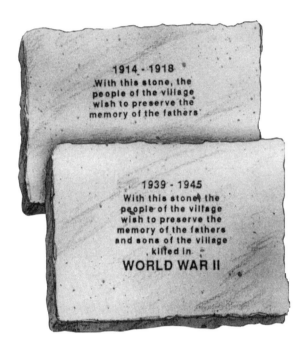

I came upon stone monuments in a small country church in England. Because these two stones have the same shape, the same type of message, and the same kind of lettering, it's easy to conclude that the text on the first stone reads "World War I." But actually, it says "The Great War." And obviously, that's the way it has to be. There can't be a World War I until there's a World War II. This reminded me of how easy it is for an author or teacher to assume that students already have an overall view of the subject being taught.

term, "paradigm shifts." (The word "paradigm" means "model.")

Perhaps the clearest example of a paradigm shift occurred when it became apparent that the macrocosmos and microcosmos could not be explained within the frame of reference of Newton's laws of physics. Einstein is the person we associate with the birth of the new paradigm, the one on which the modern relativity theory is based.

On a smaller scale, we can mention a concept that's in vogue in many companies: model-switching. Here, we're talking about organizing production, distributing responsibility among different company departments, directing and arranging the company's operations, defining markets, and much, much more. In the industry's infancy, Ford's assembly line became the model for efficient production. Things generally stayed that way up to the end of the 1960s, when other forms of organization, such as flow grouping, were introduced. We thus acquired a new model. Today it's the Japanese companies that serve as models and sources of inspiration, and this has led to the adoption of concepts like "KANBAN," "lean production," "Kaizen Kando," and "just in time."

Let's look at a company where the basic view of, say, production has been the same for many years. Everyone who works there "knows the score"—they have it down pat. If we now decide to switch to a different production model, it won't be enough to teach them to "know the new score instead," because the instructor will be teaching from a frame of reference that is different from the participants', and the result will be a clash of cultures. In a situation like this, it's absolutely essential to first determine the principles on which the old production model is based and then compare them with those of the new model.

When Alfa Laval decided to switch from a functional organization to flow grouping, the company built a small scale model of the plant to give the people involved an opportunity to discover the differences, and thus to draw conclusions about what the new form of production would mean in practical terms.

Even though this need seems obvious, people quite often fail to notice it. I've seen companies that desperately need to make drastic reductions in their lead time for developing new products—reductions that can be achieved only by adopting entirely new ways of working and cooperation. But the people in these companies are so locked into their old views and habits that the process becomes extremely slow and arduous. What's missing is a common frame of reference, a vision.

Thus, the short cut to effective learning consists in creating a bird's-eye view at an early stage—an overall context in which learners can perceive the principal relationships. Only then can we add to and flesh out the gestalt. As I pointed out earlier, the main reason why this need is so often ignored appears to be that instructors and course planners assume that learners already have the required overview. They conclude that spending a lot of time on basic understanding is ineffective, without stopping to consider that the extra effort expended in the introductory stage will pay for itself many times over by saving time and effort later.

Pedagogical editing

I don't maintain that everyone can tell a story like William Shakespeare or Milos Foreman, or that there's a Socrates or Franklin D. Roosevelt imprisoned inside every teacher just waiting to be released.

What I do maintain is that all of us, using simple tools and the same methods, can make it considerably easier for the receiver to take in information and learn.

This chapter deals primarily with being a transmitter—a teacher, lecturer, speaker, article writer, etc.—and a user of training materials of different kinds, and with how we, in these capacities, can make our presentations more pedagogical.

Richard Feynman read the following aloud from a textbook to support his criticism of university education:

Triboluminescense. Triboluminescense is the light emitted when crystals are crushed.

He proposes this explanation instead:

When you take a lump of sugar and crush it with a pair of pliers in the dark, you can see a bluish flash. Some other crystals do that too. Nobody knows why. The phenomenon is called tribuluminescense.

What's the difference?
First of all, he changes the order: the meaning first and the

term, the technical expression, last. Secondly, he replaces the abstract information given with a concrete example that lies within the reader's frame of reference and that the reader may have experienced firsthand. We can call this pedagogical editing.

What I'm saying is that the author should have done this— himself or with help from someone else—before he sent the manuscript to the printer.

The process that Feynman uses to evaluate the book's accessibility can be called pedagogical revision.

This is something I think teachers should do to determine whether a book is suitable, and/or to get an indication of how they can modify their own teaching methods to compensate for the book's deficiencies.

The reason why pedagogical editing is needed so often is that most specialists tend to base their presentation on their own logic, which in turn is based on extensive knowledge. As a result, they assume that the reader can relate individual items of information to the whole, when actually the reader first needs to have an idea of the overall context and goal (an opening) before he or she can follow and participate in the reasoning that leads to the conclusion, the knowledge. That's why many technical books are best read backwards (the last chapter first, then the next-to-last, etc).

Suppose you've written a text (article, lecture, report, letter, etc). You're satisfied with it for the most part, and normally you'd consider it finished. But you decide to see whether you can improve it pedagogically (rhetorically, dramatically). As I said, first versions of such texts usually have a structure that reflects the transmitter's way of thinking (logically) rather than the receiver's way of learning (organically).

Example 1

Let's say that the text discusses a series of measures for reducing the time a company needs to develop new products. The "logical" organization (I've seen many) usually starts with an extremely general introduction ("We live in a changing world ...") followed immediately by a description of the goals and the plan of action, which in turn is followed by a more or less detailed discussion of why we should adopt the plan of action. This may be the "logical" way to organize the presentation, but we can use

Better heading
~~Heading head~~

~~Text wordword word and texttext wordwordword. Word wordword text text~~
word word wordwordword. Texttext word wordwordword texttext word.
Wordword texttext wordwordword word word texttext wordword texttext.
More wordword and word wordwordword text text texttexttext word
wordwordword. Texttext wordwordword wordword word and texttexttext word
word text texttext wordword. Word wordwordword word text. More word
wordword texttext and text wordwordword word texttext wordword.

Texttext word and wordwordword texttext word. Wordword texttext
wordwordword word word texttext wordword texttext. More wordword word
word and wordword text text texttexttext word wordwordword. Text
wordtext and word texttext wordwordword. Word wordword text text
wordword wordwordwordword. More texttext word wordwordword texttext
word. ~~Word wordwordword word text.~~ Word wordword and texttext text
~~wordwordword word texttext wordword.~~

③ Word wordword text text wordword wordwordwordword. Texttext word and
wordwordword texttext word. Word wordwordword word text. Word word and
word word wordword text text and texttexttext word wordwordword. Text
wordtext and word. ???? *Plus some good questions*

④ Word wordwordword word text. Word word word word wordword text text
texttexttext word wordwordword. Text wordtext word texttext
wordwordword. Texttext word wordwordword texttext word. More wordword
and texttext wordwordword word word texttext wordtext. Texttext
word wordwordword texttext and word. Wordword texttext and wordwordword
word word texttext wordword texttext.

⑤ Text wordtext word and texttext wordwordword. Texttext word wordwordword
texttext word.

②
a.
Texttext word wordwordword texttext. More texttext word wordwordword and
texttext word. Wordword texttext and wordword word wordword texttext
wordword ~~texttext. Texttext word wordwordword texttext word.~~ Texttext
word wordwordword texttext. Texttext word and wordwordword texttext
~~word. Wordword texttext~~ wordword word wordword texttext wordword and
texttext. Texttext word wordwordword texttext word. Texttext word
wordwordword texttext. Wordword texttext wordword word wordword texttext
and wordword texttext. Texttext word wordwordword texttext word.
Texttext word wordwordword texttext.

① ~~Wordword texttext wordword word wordword texttext wordword texttext.~~
~~Texttext word wordwordword texttext word. Texttext word wordwordword~~
~~texttext.~~ Wordword texttext wordword word wordword texttext wordword
texttext. More ordword and texttext wordword word wordword texttext
wordword texttext. Texttext word wordwordword texttext word. Texttext
~~word wordwordword texttext. Wordword texttext wordword word wordword~~
~~texttext wordword texttext.~~

②b. Wordword texttext wordword and word wordword texttext wordword texttext.
Texttext word wordwordword texttext word. Texttext word wordwordword
texttext. Wordword texttext wordword and word wordword texttext wordword
texttext. Texttext word and wordwordword texttext word. Texttext word
wordwordword texttext.

*Suppose you've written a text (article, lecture, report, letter, etc).
You're satisfied with it for the most part, and normally, you'd consider
it finished. But you decide to see whether you can improve it pedagogically (rhetorically, dramatically).*

the pedagogical editing process to create a different structure, like this one (see the illustration on page 118):

1. Where in the text do you see an attention-getter, something that can arouse interest and curiosity? It should be provocative and get right to the point. It should give the reader/listener an idea, a glimpse, of the problem that the presentation as a whole is supposed to solve. (Example: "It takes us five years to develop a new product. Our competitors can do it in four. What is it that they do that we aren't doing—but that we could do even better?") Once you find a suitable section, and perhaps cut it down to size, place it at the front!

2. Next question: What information can be considered necessary and sufficient information for the reader/listener? Continuing with the same example, it could be a direct comparison between "what the competitor does" and "what we do." Choose the sections of the text that fit the pattern—straightforward, concrete, and simple. Be prepared to discover that some of the information is unsuitable. You may have to "kill your darlings"—to discard lines of reasoning you especially liked—but that hamper the presentation as a whole. Alfred Hitchcock, master of the thriller genre, expressed it this way: "The cost of and satisfaction over a scene you've filmed can in itself never be a reason for including that scene in the finished film." He makes a vital point. It's more important to select the things that should be included than to get hung up on what you're throwing out.

3. Then find the section or sections that will induce the reader/listener to process the information—to think! This material can be in the form of questions or statements. Example: "You've heard what the most important differences are. What do you think realistic goals would be for us with regard to each of them?" If there is no such "invitation to think" in the original text, all you have to do is add one.

4. The next step is to look for the conclusion, the whole point of the text—a section that accurately summarizes what the reader/listener has probably already surmised by now. Example: "Estimating conservatively, this is what we can achieve: . . . What this all means is that we can catch up to our competitors, and leave them behind within a mere couple of years."

5. And finally, a call for action. Example: "There's only one catch. If we don't do anything now, nothing is going to change. Here's a proposal for a plan of action."

In this way, your conclusions won't take your readers/listeners by surprise. Instead, they'll have a chance to follow and participate in a line of reasoning that will lead them to roughly the same conclusions you've drawn, step by step.

Your knowledge of what must be done becomes their knowledge of what must be done.

Similarly, you can plan a more ordinary session, like the one shown in the earlier example about how to calculate the area of a triangle. Here's a similar example, but one that can be a little harder to follow if you're totally unfamiliar with the subject.

Example 2

I've seen many variants of training in business finance. What most of them have in common is that they're more logical than pedagogical. As an example, I've chosen the "return on investments" (ROI) pyramid that I mentioned a few times earlier.

This model is usually introduced by showing an overhead (sometimes with a number of successive overlays). The lecturer then explains the meaning of each term separately, starting with "income," and then "cost of goods sold," and so forth.

After running through all of the terms, the lecturer introduces a number of economic indicators and, in the best of cases, examples of what each of them can tell us.

Pedagogical editing might then give us the following variant:

1. An attention getter: "How much interest would you earn in a year if you deposited $1000 in the bank? If you invested the same amount in our company, you'd earn no less than 14%, or $140."
2. Information: You present the model "backwards," and in each step you describe how changes affect the interest earned (the return on investment): "large surplus," "less capital," etc.
3. Processing: You ask the participants to study three companies whose financial figures over a period of years indicate different trends. Exercise: "What are the main causes behind the changes in these companies' profitability figures?" (You can even give the participants alternative answers that you've prepared in advance, and ask them to match each one to one of the companies.) This forces the participants to compare the companies' financial conditions; in other words, what percentage of revenues consists of gross margin, etc. In doing so, they're already making indirect use of economic indicators.

4. Conclusion: "These are the questions you asked, these are the relationships you studied, and these are the corresponding key indicators."
5. Application: "This is the situation of our company over the past five years. Using the economic indicators we've discussed, try to determine what our strong points and weak points are."

Believe me, it works. Even people from the finance department can get a better idea of the value of the key indicators they routinely present in their internal reports.

The next example will give you a chance to try your hand at "pedagogical editing," although within a highly structured framework.

Example 3

Let's assume that you run into a good friend who owns a car dealership with some 20 employees. He tells you that he's having problems: customers are leaving and profitability is dropping.

Now he's on his way to a meeting with his employees to, in his words, "knock them into shape." He has prepared a series of overheads that describe how he intends to make his presentation. The planned order is A, B, C, etc. Now he asks you to help him do some "pedagogical editing."

Your job is to determine which five of the right pictures you would choose, and the order in which you would arrange them. (See pages 123 and 124.) Follow the pattern presented in Example 1.

Now we´re investing in
our own training
**THE MONEY IS
THERE**
if there is a will

A. The company intends
to invest heavily in the
future.

**" lazy . . .
unfriendly
sloppy "**

E. This is what more
and more customers are
writing to us - about us ...

It´s our
COMPETENCE
=
STABILITY/KNOWLEDGE
+
EXPERIENCE

B. It's entirely up to us.

**Down with
costs**

F. With more and more
customers leaving us,
our costs are too high.

☞ Greater competition
☞ Lower margins
☞ Higher costs
☞ Lower revenues
☞ Greater customer demands
☞ Fewer customer

C. We have a trouble-
some year in front of us...

WHY?
❑ Too few personnel?
❑ Poor environment?
❑ Poor motivation?
❑ Wrong work procedures?

G. How has this situa-
tion come about?

Customers last year	800
New customers this year	80
Lost customers	250
Customers this year	**630**

800 ➡ 630

D. We've lost many
customers during the
year ...

COST EFFECTIVENESS
+
CUSTOMER BENEFITS
=
PROFITABILITY

H. The road to success
is obvious but tough.

*He has prepared a series of overheads that describe how he intends to
make his presentation: the planned order is A, B, C, etc. How would
you arrange the overheads?*

The learning process		Pedagogical editing
Interest, curiosity Mental preparedness and receptiveness.		**Exordium** "Listen..."
Information Facts and data are converted into information.		**Narratio** "This is the situation..."
Processing Information is converted into experience and insight.		**Propositio** "What do you think..."
Conclusion Experience and insight are converted into knowledge.		**Argumentatio** "Yes that's true, isn't it..."
Application Knowledge is converted into skills and attitudes - and wisdom.		**Peroratio** "And therefore..."

Start by reading through the material to see what the car dealer is trying to say. Then choose the five pictures that best convey this and arrange them in the "right" order.

Comments on Example 3: Here we can see the steps in the "pedagogical editing" process.

1. Is there anything in the text that can be used as an introduction to grab the listeners' attention and create interest and curiosity? We propose overhead E, because it will probably anger the listeners, cause protests, etc.

   (We could also start with D, which is less provocative, but the overall message is positive, so we can afford to be a little rude and critical at the start.)

2. What information is needed to keep the listeners interested and guide them towards the objective? Use the premise to help you decide which information is meaningful and which isn't. The opening overhead E will probably produce surprise, protests, excuses and, possibly, interest in how serious the problem really is. So this is a good place for overhead D: "Here's the situation in black and white."

3. Are there any questions or statements that can get the listeners to do some serious thinking? Here we suggest that the speaker not discuss his own conclusions just yet. The listeners need time to do their own reasoning. That's why overhead G fits in well here; it offers challenging questions.

   Once they're seen it, you have to give them a chance to participate seriously and discuss these questions.

4. What's the point, the conclusion, that we want the listener to understand? Apparently, the point that the speaker is trying to make (the premise) is that "if we do our jobs better, we'll be more successful in keeping our customers." That's why he placed the material that deals with this subject near the beginning of his own presentation. But if he waits until later to present his conclusion, he'll be more likely to get his listeners to agree with him. (Conclusions presented too early often have the opposite effect.) This section of the presentation is a better place for the conclusion (overhead B), because the listeners are now close to drawing the same conclusion themselves.

5. How can we reinforce the conclusion in a way that induces the employees to take appropriate action? This is the best place for A.

And the other overheads? What happened to them? The most simple answer is that they don't belong there; they don't coincide with the premise because they mix two messages (higher revenues and lower costs). It's important to stick to a single message. If the speaker had wanted to concentrate on costs instead, the presentation would have been completely different.

The learning process	Pedagogical editing	
Interest, curiosity Mental preparedness and receptiveness.	*" lazy...* *unfriendly* *sloppy"* E. This is what more and more customers are writing to us - about us ...	**Exordium** "Listen..."
Information Facts and data are converted into information.	Customers last year 800 New customers this year 80 Lost customers 250 **Customers this year 630** **800 → 630** D. We've lost many customers during the year ...	**Narratio** "This is the situation..."
Processing Information is converted into experience and insight.	**WHY?** ❏ Too few personnel? ❏ Poor environment? ❏ Poor motivation? ❏ Wrong work procedures? G. How has this situation come about?	**Propositio** "What do you think..."
Conclusion Experience and insight are converted into knowledge.	It's our **COMPETENCE** STABILITY/KNOWLEDGE EXPERIENCE B. It's entirely up to us.	**Argumentatio** "Yes that's true, isn't it..."
Application Knowledge is converted into skills and attitudes - and wisdom.	Now we're investing in our own training **THE MONEY IS THERE** if there is a will A. The company intends to invest heavily in the future.	**Peroratio** "And therefore..."

The order after pedagogical editing.

A Variant

In the three examples shown above, we started by finding the material to be presented first, and then the material to be presented next. But in some cases, its better to find the conclusion, or even the desired actions, first, and then work backwards. If we do this with Example 3 (the car dealer), the model would look like this:

a. "What do I want to achieve? Answer: "Action." So overhead A should be placed last.

b. "What conclusion or insight can lead to such action?" The answer is in B, which should thus be placed right in front of A.

c. "What discussion or thought process would probably lead to this conclusion?" G should start such a process.

d. "What information is needed to give the discussion substance?" Probably E, which shows what customers are thinking.

e. "How can I arouse the listeners' interest and make them receptive to this information?" Here D should work well.

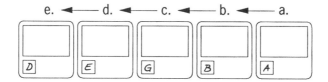

Editing backwards. Compare the results with the order shown on the preceding page.

So this method gave roughly the same results. I have no way of knowing, but I'm convinced that the author of the movie *High Noon* (see the chapter on drama) planned the entire script around the scene in which Will's wife shoots the gang leader: the odds against Will are overwhelming. Suddenly, the villain drops to the ground, shot dead. And it was Will's wife, the woman who hated violence so much, who did it.

From this scene, the author can then have worked his way backwards: how can I build up tension? How should I depict Will's conflict? How can I get the audience to take interest in this conflict? (Note here that the subject of the film isn't the

Learner-driven learning differs in a number of ways from traditional teacher-driven learning.—Instead of basing time requirements on the teaching pace...they are based on the learning pace.—Instead of being a victim of the instructor's "teaching style," each learner can make use of his or her own "learning style."—Instead of being passive spectators and listening to the conclusions of others...learners actively partici-pate and draw their own conclusions.

conflict between Will and the villains; it's the conflict between different values: to take up arms or not to take up arms.) Note also how skillfully the conflict is established in the opening of the film. In the wedding scene, Will promises to hang up his guns for good, but we as spectators soon realize that something is going to happen that causes Will to break his promise. (Will's inner conflict also appears in the film's theme music: "Do not forsake me oh my darling . . . I must face the man who hates me. . .")

These two ways (editing forward or backwards) can be used separately or together.

Even successful authors and film makers review their manuscripts this way. They often ask professional dramatists to help them "edit" their work, cut things out, change the order of the material, etc.

Obviously, you can't do any pedagogical editing if you don't have anything to edit, so you'll have to do some creative preparation first. One benefit of this technique is that you don't have to work on the content and the structure simultaneously, so you have more freedom during the creative phase to write down everything that comes to mind, spontaneously and without inhibitions.

Some people prefer to start by making notes on separate slips of paper, which they then sort and add to during the editing process. Others use mindmapping, a technique I'll discuss later.

Finally, here's a summary of the entire procedure. (You can try it yourself: start by writing a letter, memo, article, etc.)

A. Write down, spontaneously, the things you think you'd like to include. Let your thoughts flow freely; don't worry about form. Also include things you may think don't belong there; this is a good way to keep your doubts from interfering with your stream of consciousness. Moreover, you may even find that such things lead you to thoughts that later prove to be highly useful. Consider this process a kind of personal brainstorming. (In rhetoric it's called "inventio.")

B. Find a premise. See if you can find a key line of reasoning, a key sentence, or a few key words in your notes that summarize the objective of the entire presentation. This premise will serve as a signpost in the processing phase. Everything unrelated to the premise can normally be eliminated! Often, the form of a premise is "if . . . ., then. . . ." For example, "If danger approaches, then the result will be that everyone must take up arms." "If we learn what customers want, then the result will be that we can keep them." "If learners take greater interest in their training, then the result will be higher-quality knowledge." "If we opt for a different policy for buying raw materials, then the result will be shorter production time and lower costs." (Of course, these four statements refer to the examples discussed earlier.)

C. At this point we can start with the actual editing (dispositio):

1. Is there anything in the text that can be used as an introduction to "capture" the audience and create interest and curiosity?

2. What information does the receiver need in order to draw the desired conclusion? What form of information will be most likely to maintain the receiver's interest as the presentation proceeds towards the objective? Use the premise to help you decide which information is meaningful and which isn't.

3. Does this result in any questions or statements that can stimulate the receiver to think in ways that are likely to lead him or her to the objective?

4. What's the point, the conclusion, the knowledge that we want the receiver to internalize?

5. How can we reinforce this knowledge so the receiver can use it? In other words, what is it that we want the receiver to do as a result of his or her having heard or read the presentation?

D. Rewrite the text in the order marked. Make additions as necessary.

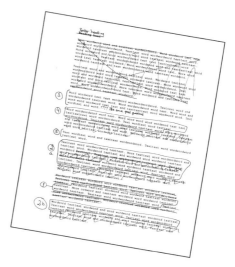

Pedagogical revision

By following the same procedure used for pedagogical editing, you can evaluate the presentations of others (course activities, video films, lesson plans, or complete course packages) in order to check their pedagogical value and decide whether, and how, they can be used.

As a teacher or instructor, you must have an idea of how pedagogically sound your course and course materials are. Instructors who are well-aware of the strengths and weaknesses of their training materials can work miracles if they know how to take advantage of and reinforce the strengths of their materials, while compensating for the weaknesses. A revision of this kind could generally follow the same pattern we described above, but preferably in the reverse order, as follows:

a. How does the author expect the new knowledge to be used? To what extent does this coincide with your own objectives?
b. What point, message, or conclusion are the participants expected to acquire in the form of knowledge?
c. Are there components that invite the learners to think—that are somehow related to the learners' prior experiences—and/or that offer opportunities for acquiring new experiences?
d. Is the information necessary and sufficient, and in suitable form?
e. How well does the material capture the learners' interest? How likely is it that they'll be involved from the start?

You can usually compensate for any weaknesses noted fairly easily by adding material of your own or, in the case of a guest lecturer, by offering him or her direct advice and suggestions for changes.

Metamessages

Pedagogical revision should also include a check for metamessages (things the author or speaker says "between the lines") that can conceivably influence learners. Here we're talking primarily about the "tone" of the presentation. Texts can also convey a kind of body language, or nonverbal messages, that infallibly reveal the author's true attitude towards his or her readers or listeners. We may not be consciously aware of metamessages, but they help to determine how receptive we are: they can make us feel insignificant and ignored, they can enrage us, and they can make us feel "stupid, incompetent, and incapable." Some commonly perceived undertones (here slightly exaggerated):

- "You don't understand this; only I can understand it."
- "If you don't understand what I mean it's your own fault."
- "Just do what I tell you without asking questions; I'll do the thinking here."
- "Don't question what I say; just listen and you'll learn something."

Here it might be a good idea to tell the story about an old fisherman teaching a famous author to sail. The dialogue goes something like this:

Fisherman: "First of all, this is a boat, get that? And this pointy thing up here at the front is called the bow. What's it called?" "The bow," repeats the author obediently. After going through the same procedure with regard to the stern, the fisherman says: "Good. Now if you want to sail close to the wind on the starboard tack. . . ." The author interrupts: "If I what?" Whereupon the fisherman noted that "if he's that dumb he'll never learn to sail." I'm sure you recognize the phenomenon.

In the same way, I've heard many experts draw the wrong conclusions about other people's eloquence and capabilities simply because these people hadn't mastered the experts' special technical language. And what's even worse, people seem to accept this and consider themselves "a dummy when it comes to economics (or whatever)." In a radio interview, a highly successful small-businessman was asked to reveal the secret behind his success. He answered, quite typically: "Well, we don't have any nifty business ideas and visions and stuff like that; we just know what customers want, and we know what we're good at, so we do it, without it costing any more than it has to." Could anyone else have said it better?

The conclusion of all this was aptly summed up by futurist John Naisbitt: "Never underestimate peoples' abilities, but never overestimate their knowledge."

In situations in which learners will be asked to work with exercises of different kinds, the method on which these exercises are based is extremely important. "The method is the message," in that it expresses an expectation of both the type of knowledge being sought, and of how this knowledge is to be used. So the method should be evaluated with this in mind.

Example

Let's say we're talking about training for the sales representatives of a computer manufacturer. If the exercises deal primarily with the technical features of the computers, the metamessage will be that these are the most important sales arguments. Thus, it would be better if the exercises concentrated on customer needs and on what customers can find of value in "our computers" as opposed to the competitors' products. In addition, it can be a good idea to make sure that the training sessions are otherwise suitable: that they're interesting, that they provide necessary and sufficient information, that they're perceived as being meaningful, that they lead to usable knowledge, etc.

Through the eyes of the learner: I've taken part in many planning meetings for courses, conferences, and seminars, and one thing that never ceases to amaze me is that these meetings often deal almost exclusively with what the instructor, the lecturer, is going to do, rather than what the learners are going to do: "First I'll talk about this or that, then you show your overheads, then I'll describe. . . ."

We can benefit if we instead take the opposite approach—if we look at things from the learner's point of view: "First they'll

Something to ponder. . .

If we wish to succeed
in helping someone to reach a particular goal
we must first find out where he is now
and start from there.

If we cannot do this,
we merely delude ourselves
into believing that we can help others.

Before we can help someone,
we must know more than he does,
but most of all,
we must understand what he understands.
If we cannot do that, our knowing more will not help.

If we nonetheless wish to show how much we know,
it is only because we are vain and arrogant,
and our true goal is to be admired,
not to help others.

All genuine helpfulness
starts with humility before those we wish to help,
so we must understand
that helping
is not a wish to dominate
but a wish to serve.

If we cannot do this,
neither can we help anyone.

Thoughts on teaching and learning from the Danish philoso-
pher Søren Kierkegaard.

hear about this or that, then they'll see your overheads, then they'll listen to my description of . . ."

The results of this kind of planning are often quite different. I've seen at first hand how the time required for a lecture can be cut in half, without losing anything, by employing this simple technique. All you have to do is put yourself in your students' place and try to develop a course that you yourself would like to take.

The Learning Process	How Will They React?
Interest, curiosity	**What do they expect?**
Mental preparedness and receptiveness.	What attitudes have they arrived with? What will they think after they've heard my introduction?
Information	**Will they listen?**
Facts and data are converted into information.	How will they reat to my choice of informations, words, examples and presentation sequence?
Processing	**How involved and active will they be?**
Information is converted into experience and insight.	Will they see any reason for working with this? Any value?
Conclusion	**What will they think they learned?**
Experience and insight are converted into knowledge.	Will they feel that it was worth the effort?
Application	**How useful will they think it is?**
Knowledge is converted into skills and attitudes—and wisdom.	Will they find parallels between this material and their own job situation? Will they use their new knowledge?

How will the participants "evaluate their training"?

Compare this with what most of us do when we're planning, say, a party. We switch on the porch light to make our guests feel welcome even before they arrive at our door. We know they need somewhere to hang their coats. We choose their places at the dinner table to ensure maximum interaction. We choose the after-dinner music with care, to get people out of their seats and out on the dance floor. And so on and so forth. In short, we plan the party through the eyes of our guests.

In the same way, you can imagine an entire training session step by step, and try to determine how the participants would react—how they would "evaluate your course."

In the last section of the book (Chapter 5), I present an evaluation form that can be used for this. The main points are shown here.

Finally, another quote from John Naisbitt that accurately describes how many learners react to the training and "internal communications" they are subjected to:

"We are drowning in information but thirst for knowledge."

Collaborative learning

On one occasion I held a lecture for a group of managers at a construction company. The room had been haphazardly converted into a conference room, with a flipchart propped against one of the long walls. The participants were sitting in a semicircle, in ordinary chairs. The atmosphere was fairly informal, but even so, something curious happened. After I'd drawn diagrams and offered explanations for perhaps half an hour, I took a short break. At that point one of the participants raised his hand and said "Excuse me, but I can't see." Not knowing quite what to say, I replied "Uh-huh?" "May I move," he asked? I looked at him a little strangely, whereupon he moved his chair a few feet and said "Thanks, now I can see!"

I often think of this episode when I take part in discussions on course formats and lesson plans, and I never quite know how to interpret it. Was this an example of a student who took responsibility by demanding better conditions for learning? Maybe, but if so, I wonder what this person, who independently makes decisions involving millions and millions of dollars every day, was doing for the first half-hour.

I've also seen the exact opposite. Early in the course, the instructor invites the students to take part in a discussion, and the most talkative among them use the opportunity to pontificate, often on the most irrelevant matters. Moreover, these discourses sometimes lead to long, drawn-out, and anything but productive discussions among a few people. The instructor may be proud of having "gotten the participants involved." But this isn't even half-true, because only a few of them are involved while the others sit there passively listening to discussions that have absolutely nothing to do with the subject at hand.

Many of the instructors I've trained have pointed out that this is a kind of Catch 22: A monologue makes the learners passive, while discussion tears the lesson plan to shreds. So what's left? (I believe that the latter experience is what compels many teachers and lecturers to revert to the monologue alternative because it at least gives him or her some control over the situation.)

There's only one other option: to get learners to collaborate and share responsibility for their instruction. (There should be no need to say it, but the fundamental purpose of teaching is to meet the needs of students.) Let me offer a parallel.

What is the typical behavior of people taking part in a reasonably productive project-group meeting with perhaps five, six, or seven participants? First of all, we know that the whole point of the meeting is that everyone understand, stay involved, and learn. That's why we can hear plenty of comments like "I didn't quite understand that; can you explain?" "Can we go back to your description and compare it with this idea?" "I don't see the connection between A and B." "If that's true, shouldn't we try something like this instead?" "Can you tell us what you did at . . . ?" "If something is unclear, we can take ten minutes to check and see whether we've all understood things the same way," etc.

In this case, spontaneous teaching and spontaneous learning dictate the participants' behavior. Even if the meeting may at times appear to be somewhat disorganized, the participants are constantly being stimulated to drive the discussion forward. This organization will work on two conditions: that the group isn't too large, and that participants have a sense of responsibility and are willing to accept responsibility. The question is: How can we create equivalent conditions in groups of 20 or 30 people that don't have a common objective driving them forward? After all, it's the learners' efforts that are important, not the instructor's.

It's almost always a good idea to split the participants up into groups of five, six, or seven people, and to place each group on its own "island" somewhere in the room. This layout gives each individual a home base where he or she can get help in understanding things that may be unclear, by discussing problems that might seem too trivial to involve the total group.

The instructor, on the other hand, can use the limited number of groups to even out differences in the participants' individual learning processes. The instructor doesn't have to spend an equal amount of time on each individual, because variations in prior knowledge, concentration, and understanding can to a great extent be absorbed and managed within the groups—if the course is arranged in a way that permits this. (The cooperation between learners, that in a traditional school setting is called cheating, can be used as a training aid.) Even in the very few cases where groups of this kind don't function the way they should (because one member is too dominant or the differences in background and values are too great, etc.), the benefits still outweigh the drawbacks. If the problems are too serious, it may be enough for the instructor to regroup the participants or talk with them about the problems.

My main point here isn't that the overall course group should be divided into smaller work groups, but doing so can be the factor that makes it possible to develop good interaction between the participants and the instructor.

The old proverb that states that "a chain is only as strong as its weakest link" is undoubtedly true, and since all learning is based on a process of advancing from insight to insight, it becomes obvious that if a learner falls behind at some stage in the learning process, what follows can easily be meaningless to him or her. A person who isn't interested won't be receptive to information; if the person is interested but the information is inaccessible then there won't be anything to process. To avoid this, we need a checkpoint at the junctures between one stage and the next.

Otherwise, what happened to one high school social science teacher can happen to us. She asked her students to write a report on euthanasia. Then, to give them some background, she spent around half an hour talking about the pain of terminal illness, the ambivalent feelings of loved ones, the ethical questions involved in taking another human life and so on and so forth. When she later started to grade the reports, she realized to her dismay that she hadn't really defined the term "euthanasia." Several of her students had written reports on youth in Asia.

Ongoing Quality Control

Let's assume we're talking about a four-hour session. If after fifteen or twenty minutes the participants don't understand the objective of the session, or aren't interested or motivated, then what follows will probably be of little value. The participants don't have access to a remote control to switch you off, so they simply switch their brain to another channel. (There is an unwritten rule that says that in a good western film, the hero, the villain, the conflict, and the scene of the action must all be introduced within the first five minutes.)

This is where the work groups come into the picture. The instructor pauses briefly and introduces a challenge or question such as "Do you recognize this problem?" The answers from the groups (or perhaps from only one group) not only give the instructor an idea of how well the participants have understood the objective, but they also help to bolster the interest of the others.

These questions followed by pauses give each individual a chance to think things through by him- or herself (just as we spontaneously pause when reading a book in order to absorb what we've read).

Teaching of the traditional kind takes many forms, but all of them have one thing in common—they shut out the people they're supposed to reach.

In the same way, we can insert a checkpoint between each natural break in the process, to ascertain the quality of the learning that has taken place.

Simple questions like these may be enough.

1. After the introduction, to check for attention and interest: "Do you agree with this? Do you recognize this?" What would you do differently if you knew how to . . . ?" "What would it mean to you personally if you could solve this kind of problem?" Another type of question: "How often do you find yourself in this kind of situation?" "What do you think the effect would be if . . . ?" Yet another type of question (that gives an indication of what's coming): "What is it that prevents you/us from . . . ?" "What would you need to know in order to . . . ?"

2. After the information stage: "So what do we have to work with?" "Is there any information you need?" (although this question can be hard to answer because there is no way of being sure whether any additional information is needed until we get into the processing stage).

3. After processing the participants' own activity: "So what conclusions have you drawn?"

4. After the transformation, when experiences and conclusions have been expressed as knowledge in fairly general terms: "What could you use this knowledge for?" "What can you do differently now that you've learned this?"

5. After the transfer, when the participants have received help in applying the knowledge in a practical situation: "What was easy? What was hard?" "What difficulties do you think you'll run into in other, similar situations?"

If the instructor doesn't allow time for such pauses and merely prattles on, then it's both reasonable and desirable for you as a student to ask for a short pause (a minute or so) if you're having problems, "to talk with the other members of the group." You'll either get help from the others, or you'll find that several of them have the same problem, and together you can ask for clarification. Failing to take such initiatives because you "don't want to embarrass/bother the instructor" is the equivalent of failing to take responsibility and, thus, of failing to try to get something out of the course.

Moreover, you'd be doing the instructor a disservice. A good friend of mine spent an entire day working with a group of Japanese students and he noted that they didn't show much interest. He mentioned this to the group's leader, who was able to explain why: "It's probably because none of them understands a word of English."

Of course, these "checkpoints" can be initiated most easily if the instructor poses questions like those I described above. But not everyone thinks that this is such a good idea. One common objection to doing so is that "students can't or won't answer questions like those honestly." That's a poor excuse, and sometimes I think the contrary is true. Instructors don't dare to ask these questions because the answers can reveal deficiencies and, most of all, "disturb the training process." When I feel like being especially nasty in such discussions, I propose that the course be run without any students at all, to avoid such disturbances completely.

But there are grounds for suspecting that some students are afraid to take responsibility. The rules of this teamwork approach are ambiguous, and old conventions (perceptions of traditional roles) make the students uncertain and apprehensive.

(I've had this experience myself: The shop workers at a large manufacturing company were invited to a course dealing with the company, leadership, and the future. A number of them called in sick the first day and didn't attend until their colleagues assured them that it wasn't "dangerous.")

Under conditions like these, it can be a good idea at the start of the course to enter into a "pedagogical contract" with the students that stipulates the conditions for learning and the rules of the game, as follows.

Pedagogical Contract

Course evaluations are a fairly common tool. Students are asked to answer a number of questions at the end of the course, to indicate what they thought was good and what they thought was not so good. Less frequently are they asked to evaluate their own efforts, which shows that the old notion that the trainer alone is responsible for the learners' instruction is still firmly entrenched.

To change this we need to do two things:

1. Evaluate the participants' efforts. In other words, the evaluation form should include questions on what the participants have done to create good conditions for learning.

2. Present and discuss the evaluation form at the beginning of the course (preferably after the introduction), in order to establish what it is that promotes learning, and to determine what the "rules of the game" are and how responsibility is to be shared.

In this way the instructor and the learners can help each other to establish in advance certain guidelines for their relations during the course. Naturally, it would help if, before doing this, the participants had a chance to learn a little about how the learning process works, to make it easier for them to determine what promotes and what hinders learning.

The student's "thank-you speech" presented on pages 72 to 75 is also available on film. It has proven to be of help in starting this process when shown at the beginning of the course. When the film is over, the instructor says that this is not the kind of thank-you speech that he or she wants to hear at the end of the course, and asks "How can we help each other to avoid that kind of outcome?" The evaluation form can then be used as the starting point for a discussion.

The result, the "pedagogical contract," doesn't have to be written down on paper, of course. It can consist merely of an agreement on how critical situations should be handled. For example:

- What do we do when somebody gets lost and can't keep up?
- What do we do when things really get boring?
- What do we do when the instructor starts "sausage-stuffing"?
- What do we do when we can't see the point of the lectures and exercises?
- What do we do when we need more time to think?
- How can we best take advantage of the knowledge and experience that the people in the group already have?
- What do we do when our experience contradicts the message of the presentation?
- How can we firmly link what we learn to our job duties and our concrete needs?
- What do we do when we'd rather have answers to questions than information related to things we haven't asked about?

To ensure that this endeavor isn't perceived as an isolated activity unrelated to the objective of the course itself, you should wait until after the introduction and then present the course content in some detail. (It isn't unusual for participants to feel insecure when the traditional training rituals are eliminated completely.)

In this way the pedagogical questions can be related directly to the planned course material, and the instructor can point out the things that he or she thinks are especially important: "Tomorrow morning we're going to have a guest lecturer who will talk about how different ways of organizing production affects tied-up asset levels, and it's important that you create a good atmosphere for her talk by not passively sitting here and letting her do all the work. How can we best prepare ourselves?"

Evaluation in Advance

The idea of sharing responsibility does not mean that you should spend a large part of the course time discussing what the course content should be and how it should be presented.

It became fashionable in the 1970s to let the participants determine the course content. Upon our arrival, we were sent out in groups to discuss "the problems we have on the job" in terms of whatever the course was supposed to deal with. After a few hours the groups' answers were presented, and we were then invited to take part in a long, drawn-out discussion on the course content and its presentation, which eventually led to a poor compromise. Our model for this was the town meeting and the leader's abdication.

What it does mean is that before each major section of the course, the instructor "puts his or her cards on the table" by describing the planned course layout, explaining how much time is going to be spent on what, listing the activities that have been planned for the participants, etc. This description can go into some detail, and can include examples of course content as well as the idea behind each component. The participants can then offer viewpoints, preferably by group, and perhaps propose a change of priorities. This provides three benefits.

First, the participants acquire what is sometimes called "preunderstanding." In other words, they get a glimpse of the whole, of the overall context, of the value of the course, that will make it easier for them to stay on the right track later. Second, it gives the instructor data for adapting and adjusting his or her plans to the prevailing conditions. Third, it provides opportunities (between longer sessions, for instance) for discussing the pedagogical contract, and for modifying it if necessary.

Lamentably, many people still haven't accepted this approach as a legitimate way of working in a training situation. "It doesn't work in practice," they say. "It's based on a

The Student's Plea Interest, curiosity	**"Here's how the course is arranged:"** The problem
"Don't stifle my natural curiosity, awaken it."	"For the next hour we're going to discuss . . ."
Information "Just give me the information I need, not a bunch of information I don't need."	**The content** "In my brief presentation I'll talk about . . . This will give you the answers to . . .
Processing "Let me think things through myself and draw my own conclusions."	**The activity** "Then you'll have the chance to work together on . . ."
Conclusion "Help me find a context for the things I've understood!"	**The knowledge** "Finally, we'll try to . . . , which means that you'll know about . . . "
Application "Help me use my knowlege, so it doesn't wither away and become useless."	**The effect** "We'll conclude by talking about how you can use what you've learned."

Prevaluation: Evaluation in advance.

romantic, idealized view of reality." What's strange is that just
a few seconds later, these very same people may use the same
method to plan a fact-finding trip to Japan: "What are our
plans? What can we see there? Wouldn't it be better to visit A
first and then B? Can't we spend more time at C so we can
learn about . . . ?"

Could it be that they simply don't believe in their
students'ability to take responsibility—a self-fulfilling
prophecy that they can then use to prove they were right?

Summary

A well-planned course should offer some margin for adjust-
ment and adaptation, to ensure that the conditions for learning
that prevail at any given time are the best possible. It should
be designed to help learners understand how the learning
process works, so they can demand more from their training
and from themselves.

It should provide conditions in which learners can take the
initiative in evaluating and influencing their training, in con-
sultation with their instructor.

Here I present three different kinds of goals. I do this
because goals that seem to be unrealistic in one situation may
very well be realistic in another. But the three have two fundamental objectives in common:

1. To give participants an opportunity to take substantial responsibility for their own efforts, and thus, their own learning;
2. To continuously help participants to learn more about their
   own learning process, so that they can develop a permanent
   ability to shoulder this responsibility.

The three kinds of goals:

1. The instructor and the learners should carry on a dialogue to
   ensure that the learners have advanced far enough in each
   stage of the learning process to make the next stage meaningful.
2. Early in the course, the learners should be given a "short lesson" on the conditions for learning. Afterwards, the instructor
   and learners should "sign a contract" in which they agree to
   work together to ensure that the conditions for learning are
   right. In concrete terms, this can be a matter of going through
   and discussing the course evaluation form that will be used at
   the end of the course: "What can we do together to make the
   evaluation score as high as possible?"

3. As a supplement to the above, the instructor should provide an introduction to and description of each major section of the course. This description can then be used as a basis for discussing how resources, primarily time, can best be used ("prevaluation" instead of mere evaluation).

Mindmapping

"Write the way you think, not the way you talk." This statement refers to a note-taking technique commonly referred to as mindmapping. Notes are an excellent memory aid, but taking good notes isn't easy, especially at lectures, meetings and, at times, when we're studying from a textbook.

Mindmapping has helped countless people the world over to organize their note taking.

When we make notes, we don't write, "Eva's home telephone number is XYZ." We write instead, "Eva home XYZ." In our agendas we don't write "Today at 12 o'clock noon I will go out and eat lunch with George Peterson." We write, "Lunch 12 George P."

To describe a company's organization, it's easier to use images than to write a long discourse. Flipcharts from meetings are often a jumble of words, circles, squares, arrows, and lines that nevertheless make sense (both when they're drawn and as a memory image) to the people who were at the meeting because shapes and colors stimulate the process of association.

The reason why so many people have problems with note taking seems to be that they're strongly influenced by written presentations in general. Even if you're "a man or woman of few words" and use abbreviations, the pattern of such note-taking is based on the conventions of written language. For example, people typically start in the upper left-hand corner and

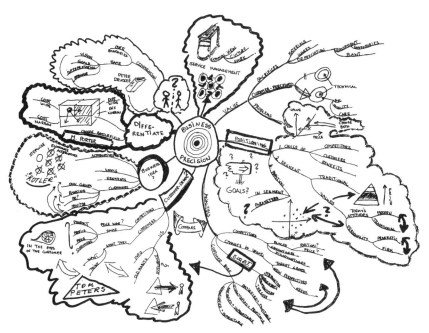

"Ordinary," linear notes and the corresponding mindmap. A mindmap is more like scribbling, a depiction of personal brainstorming, and that's the whole idea behind the technique.

continue to write, from left to right and from the top down, line after line after line. This is undoubtedly an excellent model for written language; written language is an imitation of spoken language and is, of necessity, linear—one word follows another, one sentence follows another. People in other cultures may start in a different corner of the page, but they still follow a linear pattern.

What's interesting about mindmapping is that it bypasses the linear language structure. It's based instead on our way of associating. And by now it should be clear that the brain's way of associating is anything but linear. It can best be described as organic, and that's precisely what the exhortation to "write the way you think" means: let your associations flow in all directions, and your notes will reflect this.

A great many books have been written about mindmapping, the most widely circulated of which are probably Tony Buzan's books, especially the one entitled *Use Your Head.* In several of these descriptions of mindmapping, we soon find that what the authors are really proposing is a return to the way our ancestors made notes before they had access to written language. The fact that our forefathers used images rather than words is of little interest. What is interesting is the way they organized the information—as a pattern of associations.

If you're completely unfamiliar with mindmapping, here's a chance for you to take a quick lesson. Let's take a subject that you're highly familiar with: you. And let's suppose that you're looking for a new job and are asked to present your curriculum vitae. If you use the traditional method, you start in the upper

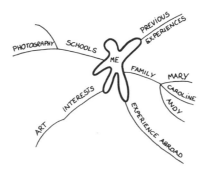

left-hand corner of the paper by writing "Name: XX," and then you add item after item of information. Even though the final version will look something like this, by doing a mindmap first, you can stimulate your thoughts and give free rein to your associations. Here's how.

Take a large (preferably around 11" × 17") sheet of white paper without lines or squares and place it in front of you with the long sides at the top and bottom. Start in the middle of the paper with a little drawing of yourself and perhaps the word "me." Tony Buzan and others recommend that we spend some time on this drawing, because it gives our brains a chance to associate and bring the subject matter into focus.

Then try making a few main branches with simple key words: "family," "schools," "interests," "previous experience," etc.

Let your associations flow and carry you forward. As soon as you think of something related to one of the main branches, make a small branch extending from this main branch and write a suitable key word on it. Your associations can jump between the main branches, and you may even come up with an association that leads to a new main branch ("experience abroad," etc.), which you can then add to your mindmap.

The result will be an extensive network that reflects your associations during the process fairly well. Include everything you can think of, even if your intuition tells you it won't form part of the final version, because irrelevant items can very well trigger new associations that will be useful. This part of the process can be likened to a kind of personal brainstorming. (Compare this to rhetoric's inventio stage.)

The next step is to "edit" your mindmap. This can be a matter of drawing arrows between some of the small branches to show that they're related to each other, or of ringing in one part of the network that you think represents an individual gestalt. Using different colors can also be a big help because they stimulate your imagination and give you a bird's-eye view of the whole. In the first stage of the editing work, you'll probably find new associations and add additional large or small branches.

Eventually, you'll have a good overview of your subject, and the task then will be to decide what information you want to

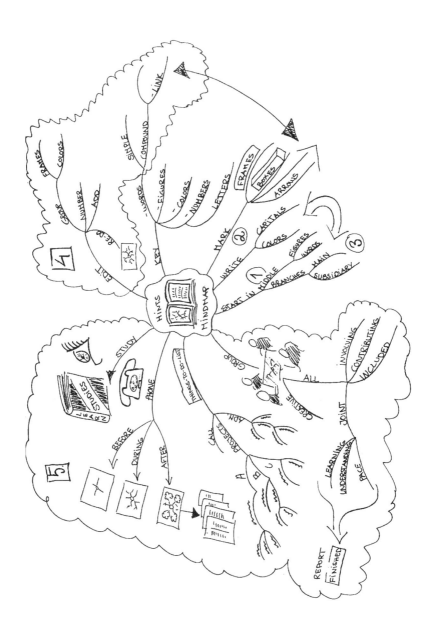

MINDMAPPING Hints

Take a sheet of white paper without lines or squares. (**11" x 17"** is a good size, but you can also use 8 1/2" x 11".) Place it front of you, preferably with the long sides at the top and bottom. Use pens or pencils of different **colors**.

Start **in the middle of the paper** with a small, simple drawing and perhaps a heading. Then make a few **main branches** and write **key words** on them. If your handwriting is hard to read, print the words in **CAPITAL LETTERS**.

Avoid writing several words on the same branch. For example, if you want to write JOB DUTIES, write JOB on the **main branch** and DUTIES on a **subsidiary branch**. In this way you leave space for new associations. You can later add other subsidiary branches with words like CONTENT, PROCEDURES, and OBJECTIVES.

Box in words or **draw figures** by things that you spontaneously feel are especially important. Remember, you're drawing a picture, not writing a text.

If things that are "logically" related wind up in different sections of the mindmap, draw arrows to show the relationship.

Also include things that at first seem to be irrelevant; they can trigger new associations.

If you get stuck, choose a key word at random. (Place your finger anywhere in the text and choose the closest noun or verb.)

Continue adding to your mindmap until you feel that you've gotten a good part of your ideas down on paper.

Edit Your Mindmap

One good way is to **bring in** related thoughts preferably using a different color for each type.

Insert numbers, to indicate the order of importance, or to indicate a suitable order for a possible presentation.

Make additions to your mindmap— new branches, key words, and drawings—as new associations pop up.

Other uses:

For phone discussions, prepare by mindmapping for a few minutes to ensure that you don't forget any critical items. Add to your mindmap during the conversation so you can use it later as a "transcript" of the discussion.

A large part of the stress we are subjected to on the job is the result of uncertainty as to what is most important and, at times, a fear of forgetting important items. Draw a mindmap of what you have to do. With the mindmap in front of you, you can then plan and set priorities without pressure.

Mindmapping is an excellent way to stay in control in a study situation. (More on this in the next chapter.)

At meetings, thought processes can be stimulated by "throwing a flipchart on the table" and letting everyone contribute to a joint mindmap.

include in your curriculum, and how it should be arranged. Obviously, the simplest way is to number the branches that you think are relevant, in the order you find most suitable, taking into account the principles of pedagogical editing I discussed earlier. (Compare this to rhetoric's dispositio stage.)

Once this is done, all you have to do is sit down at a word processor or with a dictaphone and decide on the wording.

Many lectures draft their presentations this way, and then use their mindmaps as cue cards. A lot of people prepare for telephone conversations by making a simple mindmap on their note pads and then filling in new keywords as the conversation progresses. Notes taken at meetings in this manner make it much easier to remember later what actually happened at the meeting.

This technique is also invaluable as a study aid.

I've summarized the most important mindmapping principles on the page 151.

The most important benefit of mindmapping is that it stimulates the association process. Moreover, there's a place in the mindmap for every thought that appears. Mindmapping is a way to separate the creative thought process (mindmapping itself) from the writing process (the final manuscript). Normally, these two processes—the free association of thoughts and the formal requirements of structure and linguistics—constantly interfere with each other.

Another significant benefit is that a mindmap is much easier to decipher later than traditional notes. The visual pattern, reinforced by colors and figures and arrows, makes it easier for the brain to return to the situation in which the mindmap was created. Linear notes seldom offer this opportunity, and occasionally people even have trouble remembering what their abbreviations mean. The fact that mindmapping is superior to traditional, linear note taking at lectures should be irrefutable, but many people argue that not even mindmapping can help them to take good notes at lectures. If you're one of these people, it may be better to be less ambitious, and accept the fact that your notes look more like a collection of disconnected doodles. But then give yourself five to ten minutes after the lecture to "compile" these doodles, which may cover several pages, into a mindmap of the most important items.

In this way, mindmapping will help you to "relive" the learning experience and deepen your learning, and thereby enable you to take better advantage of opportunities for acquiring permanent knowledge.

Finally, by helping to draw a single mindmap, all of the participants in development meetings of different kinds can contribute to the discussion—and create a joint document at the same time.

The art of studying

One day a colleague of mine sat idly leafing through a fairly thick, newly released book on strategic planning. I asked him what he was looking for. "I won't know until I find it," he replied coolly. The ways we approach a technical book can be roughly classified into four categories:

1. We know exactly what information or knowledge we're after and we go straight to it. We usually use this approach with user instructions, some manuals, and the telephone book.

2. We know that the book contains descriptions and explanations of things we want to learn about, so we use the table of contents to find them and we concentrate on the sections of interest. We know what our questions are, and now we set out to find the answers. ("What proteins are active in the blood coagulation process?" "How do you calculate the mean maintenance interval for a machine?")

3. We're interested in the book's topic, but we don't quite know what we can get out of this particular book. In any case we decide to give it a chance and start to read it.

4. For some reason, we feel that people expect us to read this
   book, and that we may even have to prove in one way or
   another that we've read it. So we're more interested in comply-
   ing with expectations/demands than we are in the book itself.

This chapter is dedicated to those who recognized themselves
in categories three or four, and who want to get more out of
such books—but with less effort.

People who read a lot and have a solid knowledge of a subject
can effortlessly read several books on that subject every week.
They've gradually developed their spontaneous learning
process, and they approach a book in an entirely different
way than do people that lack this expertise. How do they do
it?

The art of studying effectively is partly a matter of training
and partly a matter of technique. If this is important to you, I
suggest you pick out a suitable technical book and confront it
as described below. One or a couple of such experiences will be
enough for you to learn the technique; the rest is training.

But first, a few words about the prerequisites, mainly about
old habits that you may need to change.

All reading is a dialogue between the author and the reader.
Novelists know this and write accordingly. On the other hand,
the desire of technical book authors to be complete tends to
shut the reader out of the dialogue. The result can easily
become a monologue that provides few, if any, opportunities for
reflection.

As I said earlier, experts tend to arrange their presentations
according to the way they think rather than the way the reader
learns. This manner of writing causes problems for people who
are in the habit of reading a technical book roughly as they
would read a novel (starting on page one in the upper left-hand
corner). Reading a book this way leaves all decisions related to
the learning process in the hands of the author.

Few technical books are written well enough to make this
method of studying the most effective method. In other words,
it isn't a good idea to read a technical book from cover to cover.
Nor is it necessary, as we'll see.

If you try to read a technical book from cover to cover, you'll
most likely get bogged down in convoluted lines of reasoning

over and over again. If you don't give up altogether, you'll have to make an enormous effort to overcome the obstacles. The alternative is to read less "obediently," to skip over the hard parts and read on, and return to the hard parts later, after you've gotten additional information from the easier parts. "Do it the way you'd do a jigsaw puzzle," says Tony Buzan in his book *Use Your Head*. This, in a few words, is Buzan's main idea (which we alluded to earlier): when we put a jigsaw puzzle together, we don't start in the upper left-hand corner and then try to fit each piece in the right order. We instead put all of the edge pieces in place first, to form the frame. Then we assemble each conspicuous gestalt (a church tower, mountain peak, or whatever) separately, and fit it tentatively into the main picture. When the gestalts are large and numerous enough, it becomes easy to put several of them together to form larger units, until finally, we can see the entire picture (the total gestalt), even though only half of the pieces are in place. If all of the remaining pieces are blue and make up the sky in the picture, there's really no reason for us to continue if all we want to do is know what the contents of the picture are. In fact, it may have been possible for us to stop much earlier.

In the same way, says Buzan, we can approach a technical book by first getting an overview (the frame), and then searching for easy-to-understand messages (gestalts) that we can successively put together to form larger units.

We can express this another way. If the author hasn't succeeded in editing his manuscript pedagogically, we can pedagogically edit our way of approaching the book. Obviously, it should be the learning process that determines how you study.

Step by Step

I suggest you first read the text below, and then use the checklist that follows it (on pages 160 and 161) when you're ready to come to grips with your technical book.

1. Get interested!   This advice isn't as strange as it seems. Like my colleague leafing through his technical book to find something usable, first get an overview and work up some interest. Thumb through the book and concentrate on headings and pictures. See if you can associate the pictures and captions with things within your own range of experience. Place small "flags" (bookmarks, etc.) wherever you find something interesting, after writing a key word or two on them. (Compare this with the way people approach a buffet table: those with experience go around the table once with their empty plate, whetting their appetites by mentally "tasting" different combinations.)

Then take a short break, preferably with a note pad in your hand, and think about situations in which you could conceivably make use of whatever you think you can get out of the book. What you're actually doing now is creating your own "opening" by searching for the book's premise. Suppose that the title of the book is simply *Strength of Materials*. What good would it do you to read it from cover to cover (unless you're trying to pass a test)? In any case, when you start leafing through the book you'll most likely run into something that attracts your attention, and you'll also get a general idea of what the book has to offer. This is precisely what we all do when we're out sightseeing in an unfamiliar city. When we come to the town square, we stop and look around. We're bombarded with impressions, and we unconsciously ask ourselves, "What can I get out of this?" The difference between the book and the square is that the square "presents itself," while you have to leaf through the book in order to get a similar overview.

In the unlikely event you don't succeed in working up any interest and, more important, you can't find any direct relation to a practical application, make one up! For example, decide that "tomorrow I'm going to tell the people at work about the main points of this book," or "I'm going to write a two-page summary of this book and give it to my boss."

In doing so, you prepare yourself mentally—on your own terms and in a way that's based on your own experience and your own situation. Thus you've entered into a dialogue with the author, even though he or she may not have invited you. But what's most important here is that you're still the one who's in charge.

2. Look for usable information.   It's usually enough to read the introduction and conclusion of each chapter, because authors of technical books tend to start with, "In this chapter I intend to. . ." and/or conclude with, "In this chapter I have discussed. . . ."

If this doesn't work, start by reading roughly the last quarter of each chapter, since the main points of the chapter usually wind up there. (You can even try this when reading newspaper articles, cultural articles, editorials, etc. If it looks interesting, back up a little, etc.)

You may wonder if, by reading this way, you won't miss the logical sequence of the presentation, but that's the whole point here: the brain has no trouble sorting information and creating gestalts, regardless of the sequence in which the information is presented. On the contrary, this way of searching for information provides more associations with what you already know. That's precisely what you need to keep your learning process running at full speed.

While you search, continue to jot down key words on small pieces of paper that you can use as bookmarks. Continue also to make notes (a mindmap) on anything you find interesting.

3. Look for relationships that enable you to draw conclusions. Add more information as necessary. Now it's time for another break, a chance to just sit back and think. What conclusions have you drawn so far? What's the difference between what you knew before and what the author is trying to teach you?

You may find that important "pieces of the puzzle" are still missing, but if you use your bookmarks, you can easily go back to the book and look for them. Another way of finding further information is to look at other presentations on the same subject. They can provide additional associations that support conclusions and understanding.

4. Compare your conclusions with the author's. Correct as necessary. Continue this way until you think you've understood what the author is saying, and then compare your own conclusions with those the author has presented. Do they agree?

If not, note the differences and try to understand the reasons for them.

For example, you may quite often agree with the author "in principle." You may even feel that all of the author's conclusions are highly obvious, and that all you've really gotten out of

your study of the book is an orderly list of what you already
"knew." (For example: "In order to achieve optimum quality, it
is essential that everyone involved understand that for us, all
of the things that our customers value constitute rigorous
demands, and that the forms of leadership adopted by the company are designed to stimulate employees to act accordingly.")

This statement won't really mean anything to you until
you've thought about what concrete changes would be needed
in your own activities in order to achieve this "obvious" objective. Don't let the author's highly general and somewhat
abstract way of reasoning tempt you into being abstract. Your
contribution to the dialogue between you and the author is
your own experience, your own knowledge, and your own
needs.

**5. Use your new knowledge in a simulated situation.
Add more knowledge as necessary.**   Today's athletes practice "seeing" the entire course of a pending race or match, step
by step, as if a film of the event were being projected onto their
retinas. This exercise "programs" their brains for the desired
form of behavior. You can try it yourself on the way to your
office. Let's suppose you're going to meet someone, and you
know you have to get some keys out of the top drawer of your
desk first. If you're afraid of forgetting the keys, it can help to
mentally "run the film." ("I open the door, go straight to my
office, open the drawer, see the keys, pick them up, put them in
my pocket, squeeze them until my hand hurts," etc.) When you
then arrive at your office, your associations will help you
remember what you did in your imagination—your brain "won't
be satisfied" until it has registered that feeling in your hand.
This technique is called "imaging," and it determines to a great
extent how useful your newly acquired knowledge will be to
you.

The idea is that the knowledge has to "be there when you
need it." Let's say you read a book about child rearing that says:

> It is better to give the child encouragement on how to behave than
> instructions on how not to behave. Otherwise, the child's attention
> will be focused on the wrong behavior rather than the right behav
> ior. For example, we have noted that young, inexperienced bicycle
> riders tend to run into obstacles because their attention, their fear,

is intensely focused on the obstacle as such, while more experienced riders concentrate on avoiding the obstacle. Consequently there is no conflict between their attention and their actions.

You think this makes sense. But the following day at the dinner table your son drops food on the table from his spoon and you say, "Try not to get food on the table."

If, as you read this book, you'd imagined the situation at the dinner table, and "programmed" yourself to behave a certain way in that situation, your associations would have induced you to say instead "Try to keep your food on your spoon."

Psychologists differentiate between what they call semantic memory and episodic memory. (Both of these types are classified as long-term memory.) Episodic memory can be described as the memory of events, and it involves a large number of associations: face, smells, lights, sounds, and emotions. In semantic (linguistic) memory, most of these associations are absent. That's why it's easier to remember (recreate) events than statements. From this we get the classic expression: "I hear and I forget; I see and I remember; I do and I understand." We can use imaging to place typical episodes in our semantic memory and make them much more accessible.

The famous psychologist Jean Piaget long had a vivid memory of an attempt to kidnap him when he was a child. Not until he was well into adulthood did Piaget learn that his nursemaid had made up the whole story. His imagination had created an episodic memory based entirely on a semantic memory.

The conclusion we can draw from all of this is really fairly simple. Perhaps all we have to do is think for five minutes about various concrete situations in which our new knowledge can be useful. By using our imaginations to simulate ways of using such knowledge, we can create episodic memories that will be relatively easy to access when we later find ourselves in similar situations. It also depends on how you started your reading—on whether you managed to get interested, and on your perception of the possible benefits.

When you get this far you may find that you've read only a fourth or a fifth of the book, but nonetheless have absorbed everything of value the book had to offer in a pleasant and effective way. As I said, try to follow this model fairly systematically once or twice. See the summary on the following pages.

You'll gain valuable experience that will enable you to take on any technical book in a way totally unlike the standard cover-to-cover method you may have used in the past.

Summary

1. Get interested!
   * Leaf through the book.
   * Study only headings and pictures.
   * Write key words on "flags" that you can use as bookmarks.
   Then:
   * Think about situations in which the subject discussed in the book could be of use to you.
   * Make notes.
   * If you don't see any immediate use for the knowledge, make one up (a lecture, a two-page summary, a letter to a friend, etc.).
2. Look for usable information.
   * Read the introduction and conclusion of each chapter.
   * If necessary, read the last quarter of each chapter.
   * Continue to jot down key words on bookmarks and to make notes.
3. Look for relationships that enable you to draw conclusions. Add more information as necessary.
   * Search for relationships, conclusions, gestalts.
   * Look for and add missing information as necessary.
   * Write your conclusions down on paper.
4. Compare your conclusions with the author's. Correct as necessary.
   * Study the author's conclusions and compare them with your own.
   * Compare the conclusions with your own practical experience and note both similarities and differences.
5. Use your new knowledge in a simulated situation. Add more knowledge as necessary.
   * Imagine various situations in which you can use the knowledge. Imagine also what the results would be.

What are the elements here? Study the headings, pictures, charts—everything *except* the main text.

Try to find the "contours." Look through the introduction and conclusion of each chapter. Mark the interesting things with bookmarks.

Ask questions, look for links—"meaningful wholes."

Look for the remaining parts: What are your conclusions? What are the author's conclusions?

Transform your knowledge into useful skills—"when," "where," "how."

Study the same way you'd do a jigsaw puzzle.

Other ways

O n one occasion I was asked by a company to create a
course on assets management. After doing the preliminary work I realized that offering such a course would
be fairly meaningless. I found that the company's financial
information system was set up in a way that rewarded the
wrong behavior. For example, the performance evaluation for
purchasing managers was based on their ability to get the
biggest discounts, and not at all on whether they helped to
reduce tied-up capital. So for them, buying the largest quantities possible to obtain the maximum discount was the logical
thing to do. No assets management course was likely to change
their behavior. I suggested instead that the information
system (and thus the reward system) be revised, and that no
real training was necessary, because the purchasing managers would automatically adapt their behavior to the new
system.

With this brief example I'm trying to draw attention to the
"teaching aids" available outside the classroom. Our everyday
surroundings contain many such tools.

An aluminum plant was having quality problems. The company invested a great deal of time and effort in training. But
the improvements were marginal until one day it suddenly
occurred to somebody to wash the skylights, which were coated
with years of grime. The quality level immediately skyrocketed.

Other examples include job rotation, and measures like
allowing people to spend some time "practicing" in a department other than their own. Similarly, participation in development projects of different kinds can be a substitute for training
of a more conventional nature. The same is true of changes in
the forms of cooperation being used.

Another clear trend in today's companies is that the development of expertise has become important to everyone, and it
forms an integral part of our everyday work. That's why the
role of the training department is also changing—from merely

being the company's "course institution" to serving as consultative support for line supervisors.

An important result of this trend is that the ways of identifying and expressing training needs have also changed—from "a need for courses" to "a need for specific experiences."

As we'll soon see, this new way of thinking has also prompted people to reconsider their traditional view of company training activities.

5.

The power of learning

The burden of proof for
demonstrating
the effects of training should rest
primarily on the one trained
or the learner:
The value of knowledge can only be
measured by the person
possessing it.

The burden
of proof

For anyone who falls overboard from a boat, knowing how to swim is invaluable. As a way of enriching leisure time, it's worth much less, and as an aid in cooking, it's of no value at all.

So trying to determine the value of knowledge can only lead to philosophical reflections. All the same, it's important to be aware of the value of certain knowledge when determining training needs and when deciding how too meet them. It's in this context that the contents of this section should be viewed.

Obviously, the value of knowledge for a company is directly related to productivity and business activities. In accounting terms, we can express it like this: Material is purchased for $100. Labor is used to process it into a product. If the labor costs amount to $200, then the value (the book value) of the product is $300. If a customer is willing to pay $350 for the product, then the value is $350. We can call this the customer value.

Everything a company does to develop the capabilities of its people can be related to these two values—the book value (costs) and the customer value (price). And these values reflect the two main objectives of management: to reduce costs and to increase the price/value (through better service, better quality, better delivery capability, etc.).

One problem is that these two major efforts seem to contradict each other, because we've learned to view costs as a necessary evil. The atmosphere in a company that concentrates on cost-cutting is completely different than that of an enterprise that stresses renewal, investment, the improvement of service, and quality. The first-mentioned attitude is more prevalent during hard times and is perceived as a defensive tactic, while the latter, which is more common when times are good, is viewed as an offensive strategy.

We're all familiar with this, as we are with the difficulty of doing both things at the same time. The attitude toward costs is firmly established. That's why it's interesting to study companies that have succeeded in increasing the customer value of their products while holding the corresponding costs at the same level, or even reducing them.

It appears that people in such companies have learned to look at costs differently. Each cost dollar is viewed as a resource for creating profit. Then the question is no longer "how can we avoid costs," but rather "where can the costs do the most good." This is the constructive significance of the term "resource allocation" or "cost allocation." Looking at costs this way, the apparent conflict between "lower costs" and "increased customer value" disappears.

The challenge, the premise, will be clear-cut and will contain no real contradictions: "if we learn to use our limited resources where they can do the most good, our profitability—and our resources—will increase."

(This coincides with the trend to replace the term "cost consciousness" with "business sense." It's interesting to note here that even though many companies pay lip service to the principles of the market economy and consider market forces as the best regulator of cost/value, their internal structure is based on the tenets of central planning. This situation is now changing.)

All needs that involve training (and other forms of competence development) can thus be related to the ability to use resources (capital and know-how). And all training can be evaluated on the basis of the added value it creates by enabling resources to be used differently.

An example: let's suppose that a sales representative gets orders from an average of 10 percent of the customers he or she visits. Question: what can be done to increase that percentage? One answer could be "to visit a better selection of customers." This will require that the sales representative have better knowledge of the selection criteria. Suppose also that this will require a shift to a more demanding customer segment, where the competition is more aggressive.

To succeed, the sales representative will have to learn more about how these customers think, and about the benefits of the company's product that these customers can consider important in terms of the way they make their choices.

Let's say we estimate that these efforts can lead to an increase in successful visits amounting to a couple of percentage points. The result would then be a sales increase of 10 percent to 20 percent, and the value of such an increase can be measured.

Here is another example. At a certain company, the designers develop a new product first. Then the production engineers take over and decide how the product should be manufactured. During this process, the production engineers have to go back to the designers many times to discuss design changes needed to make the production process more efficient. This not only takes time; it also results in a waste of both groups' resources.

Questions: Would it be possible for the designers and production engineers to start working together at an earlier stage of the project?

What would the value of such a change be if the change resulted in a reduction of the overall time required, a reduction in resource waste and, perhaps, the creation of better designs?

What additional expertise could probably be necessary and sufficient to make this change in resource use feasible?

In both cases it's relatively easy to determine the potential value of the change. But what I'm saying is that the same kind of reasoning should precede training of all kinds.

Sweeping, general conclusions like "they have to learn more about finance" or "broad training in total quality wouldn't hurt" aren't enough. What we need is a reasonably good idea of what behavior we want to change, a notion of the probability of achieving such a change, and a rough estimate of its value.

I purposely use words like "idea," "notion," and "estimate" because I believe more in well-grounded but inexact evaluations than in presumably precise number juggling.

These things are obvious, but I spend a lot of time on them because I've learned through many years of experience that, in practice, people seem to have difficulty identifying and taking stock of training needs this way. The training specialists have the insight; that's not where the problem lies. It lies in large part with the customers for training—management, department heads, and the trainees themselves. This will not seem so strange if we remember that matters related to acquiring expertise have been left in other people's hands for decades.

One important step in the right direction would be to cut down on discussions about knowledge needs in terms of course content, and to dedicate much more energy to determining what changes in behavior (and in resource use) are needed.

"Starting with project X, we want our designers and production engineers to start working together right from the design stage, and to take joint responsibility all the way up to the finished product."

"We want our sales people to choose the customers they visit with greater precision and thought."

In this way, "management's goal" can also be "the learner's goal."

"I want to study our current customer base to get a better idea of what the common denominators are for the customers who choose us rather than our competitors."

Tangible ideas about desirable, concrete changes in the company's operations are the only reasonable grounds for establishing training needs and for finding ways of satisfying those needs.

I've encountered different reactions to this idea. Some people say that this line of reasoning is too narrow, almost cynical. I personally believe that it's more cynical to waste people's time by teaching them things they don't understand or that are of no real use to them.

But at the same time, I fully realize that there are many examples of valuable training that aren't easy to relate directly to desired changes in the company's operations—courses, seminars, and conferences, where the benefits can't be perceived in advance. But even in these cases, the course layout and the trainees' participation in the course can be improved if everyone, separately or together, decides on an objective. It can be as simple as "getting an idea of what we should do more of and less of to better meet customer demands, give the other departments better service," etc.

Look at it like this: the burden of proof for demonstrating the value of training should rest primarily on the training customer or the learner. This is no more unreasonable than placing the burden of proof for demonstrating the value of a new machine on the buyer. Obviously, the supplier must provide a product that has the desired characteristics, but in the final analysis, it's the user of that product who decides its value.

In other words, the value of knowledge can only be measured by the person possessing it.

Quality

What's the difference between a good course and a poor course? On one occasion I happened to hear the following conversation: "Was the course any good?" "I guess so." "What did you learn?" After some delay: "I don't know, I forgot!"

This dialogue reveals a couple of interesting attitudes. The student "guesses" that the course was good and thus fails to include himself and his own perception of the course in his evaluation, even though he invested both time and effort. "Forgot" implies that the learner didn't find anything of real, practical use in the course; the benefits appear to be negligible. (With regard to what other investment would an equivalent dialogue be acceptable? "Is that new machine you bought any good?" "I guess so." "What good is it?" "I don't know.")

The challenge consists of encouraging and helping the learner demand more in terms of overall quality from his or her training.

For decades, people in management have made enormous efforts to measure the value of the training being provided. While it's true that the emphasis has varied over the years (and with changing economic conditions), the methods used have been fairly similar.

1. Measuring results, in the form of knowledge that the learners can display at the end of the course. The criteria are the established cognitive objectives, and the results are measured using some sort of final exam or test of knowledge.

This method has two main weaknesses. First of all, it assumes that the correct cognitive objectives have been chosen—which isn't always true. Second, it assumes that there is a connection between the quality of the knowledge the learners can display at the end of the course and their ability to use this knowledge in practice—which is true even less often.

For example, a person may have knowledge of different business strategy models, but this doesn't say very much about that person's ability to act strategically.

Critics call this the black-box view. This expression has its origin in the criticism of psychological and pedagogical research in the late sixties. The critics pointed out that researchers viewed the human brain as a black box: you stuff something in one end and study whatever comes out the other end, without any real interest for what happens inside the box. That's why efforts are being made to replace cognitive tests with exercises involving practical situations of different kinds (simulation, role playing, problem solving), which in turn correspond to the situations in which the new knowledge is supposed to leave its mark. In addition, well-planned exercises directly related to the company's operations (often in the form of project work) are being used increasingly.

As a result, we can evaluate the quality and usefulness of the knowledge, not just the quantity, while giving continued learning and internalization a chance. In this way, everyone involved gets help in evaluating the outcome of the training— the "true" (subjective) value of the knowledge. This is precisely what happens in programs like "action learning," "experiential learning," and "collaborative learning," in which the forms of work themselves require the measurement of results as described.

2. Measuring the learners' evaluation of their training. Here an evaluation form is used. It contains questions like those we see in airline surveys of customer satisfaction. What the main question in these forms really asks is, "How satisfied are you with our way of giving you training?" These questions reveal a traditional idea about instructor/student roles, namely that the instructor provides training which the learners consume. Responsibility for the value of courses lies entirely with instructors and course planners.

In my view, the weakness of this method is that it easily leads to the wrong conclusions. Even if a theatrical production is skillfully staged, that doesn't automatically mean the play will be a success; if a member of a group tour to Europe sits in his or her hotel room and gripes, that doesn't automatically mean that the tour was poorly arranged.

We've all heard management people say, "We fully support the company's training efforts. . . . The development of know-how is a vital factor in our company's future growth. . . . People are our company's most important resource. . . ." Unfortunately, all too often it turns out that the support they're talking about really means that they "let it happen." This is most noticeable in hard times, when the training budget is usually one of the first items to be slashed. In such a situation, statistics about the number of satisfied course participants won't help.

A belief that training of different kinds has little effect in the short term must lie behind this attitude. The same tendency can be seen in companies' advertising. When times are good their ads focus more on the long term, "We take care of you," and on the company's mission, its values, and its role in the community. In hard times the ads are more product/sales-oriented, "buy, buy, buy."

In short, people don't seem to believe that the effects of training can be perceived immediately, that training can be a method for achieving desired short-term changes.

But attitudes like these are also changing. One sign of this is that responsibility for training is being moved closer to the line (directly under the marketing manager, for instance). In addition, the development of expertise is finally becoming a matter for upper-level management. In many cases, this can be traced to the fact that product reliability (which, in turn, depends on know-how) is rising and becoming an increasingly important competitive factor, but a more common result is that, as a company strives to minimize its work force, it becomes more dependent on those who are left.

In any case, the primary goal has been to measure the effects of training in the company's operations, as discussed earlier. A great deal has been written about how important this is, but fairly little about how to do it. The only reasonable thing to do is to start with what a person was hired to do, and then determine whether training can help that person to do it better. In companies that keep track of their employees' performance on a fairly continuous basis, such records are the obvious place to find out what effects a certain type of training has had.

The problem is that most companies don't perform such evaluations systematically, and when they do, the tools used are often blunt and primitive. The extremely wide variation in interest and participation in performance appraisals between supervisors and workers shows the difficulty of this process.

If workers' performance isn't evaluated regularly according to some systematic model, I can't for the life of me understand how changes in their performance can be measured. That's why I believe we have to have a solid idea in advance of how the results of training will affect the company's operations, and then try to find out afterwards whether what we thought would happen actually happened.

There's no reason to treat training any differently than other investments: we note a concrete need, we search for alternative solutions, we compare them in terms of the relation between benefit (value) and effort (time and cost), and we make a decision.

If the one trained (manager/learner) can't make this judgment, who can?

The only problem here is that many managers and workers haven't been very successful in identifying the longer-term needs for developing expertise. But even this is changing, primarily for three reasons.

First, people today demand much more when it comes to their personal development, so they're much more receptive to the opportunities that training and other forms of professional development offer.

Second, the conditions that companies must adapt to are changing faster and faster, which means that impulses to study the need for greater expertise are coming at shorter and shorter intervals.

Third, even though companies are clearly tending to centralize decision making on matters that affect the company as a whole, there is at the same time an even clearer tendency to decentralize responsibility for everyday operations. As such responsibility increases, the responsibility for ensuring that the necessary expertise is available increases as well.

This trend has led to a badly needed overhaul of many companies' training departments. As a training department manager expressed it, "We've finally gotten customers who know what they want."

Just as for all other goods and services, the customer is the final arbiter of value. Just as for all other goods and services, the customer decides who offers the most value for money.

In summary, the most important criteria for evaluating the overall quality of training are:

1. the usability of the knowledge in creating identifiable added value in the company's operations,
2. the magnitude of the effort (time/lost production, personal dedication, money) needed to acquire this knowledge,
3. the time that elapses from the instant the need is discovered until the knowledge starts to benefit the company.

The same criteria can be used to draw up a "requirement specification" for a certain type of training, and to evaluate already existing training. The existence of a specific "solution" helps the "customer" to identify and formulate his or her problems or needs more precisely.

The same is true when we buy a computer program. Twenty years ago, the user had to provide a detailed description of the desired program functions before the systems analyst even started. Today, the customer is more likely to study existing designs first, as an aid in understanding what features he or she can and should demand: "I didn't know what my problem was until I found a solution to it."

The first criterion (the usability of the knowledge) requires that both the customer and the supplier see the connection between knowledge of a certain subject and of a certain quality on the one hand, and the probability of a certain desirable behavior on the other. For example, it's more likely that a person will be able to ride a bike after discovering for him- or herself how to ride a bike than it is if he or she just learns the theory behind how a bike works and the names of the different parts. Sales people are likely to change their priorities if they discover that certain types of prospects are more likely to buy than others. The same sales people will probably do a better job if they learn to visualize the customer's decision-making process, and to determine in advance how their sales arguments will be received by customers. People are more likely to act more strategically if they can experience the consequences of different strategies in a given situation. Evaluating according to this criterion means judging whether the intended knowledge (content and quality) will increase sufficiently the probability of achieving the desired behavior. As Peter Drucker says:

> Books contain information; whereas knowledge is the ability to apply information to specific work and performance. And that only comes with a human being, his brain, or the skill of his hands.

For the second criterion (magnitude of the effort), the concept of productivity (benefit/value in relation to effort/cost) can be used to compare alternatives. If you want to go further and study the potential for a higher level of productivity (greater benefit, less effort), you must determine the extent to which the necessary conditions for learning exist.

I'm referring here to the conditions for learning I discussed earlier. A tool for such an evaluation is presented in the closing section. Of course, this criterion also includes an evaluation of the additional personnel resources that become available as a result of the shorter training time required.

The third criterion (total time required) should be self-explanatory, but for the sake of thoroughness, we can point out that it isn't difficult to calculate the value of, say, launching a product earlier, and thus, reaching full production capacity at a new plant faster.

Moreover, the accelerating pace of change has made it necessary at least to finish with one effort before starting another. The old model for change, "unfreeze, change, refreeze," is no longer valid to the same extent that it was before. A more suitable model for today's needs is "unfreeze, change, change, change. . . ."

The overall time needed to carry out an action can also be important in terms of impact: if a message reaches many people in a company at the same time, the total effect in some cases will be much greater than if such efforts are spread out over a period of time.

For one thing, people will tend to see themselves as part of a team effort rather than as mere cogs in a machine, and this obviously has a good effect on attitudes.

For another, the effect will be greater because the force will be concentrated. If one hundred people pull on a rope at the same time, the force will be greater than if one person pulls the rope once a day for one hundred days.

Needs

A few years ago we received a commission from a food company that was having quality problems in production and in the supporting (administrative) departments. Our job was to produce training material of the type used in quality circles.

We came up with a solution in which the supervisors, using this material, would train the people working under them.

We felt that this was a good idea, because training should be one of a supervisor's most important tasks. We also decided to use this method to achieve several of the benefits I've discussed earlier.

To ensure that the supervisors/instructors would know precisely what their task was, we invited them to a run-through of the material, a kind of train-the-trainer seminar, which took a little over half a day. But I don't intend to talk about the seminar itself; what is interesting is what happened the evening before. We had met with the company's CEO to discuss how he would introduce the seminar.

He felt this was fairly obvious, and suggested an introduction something like this:

> Before we get started, I just want to take this opportunity to tell you that these activities have my complete support. If you have any problems, don't hesitate to contact one of the management people, and we'll do what we can to help you. For you, your

subordinates and the company, it's vital that this program be a resounding success.

Those of us in the project group didn't think this was the right message, and the introduction turned out to be more like this:

> We've asked all of you to come here today because we have to do something about quality. Within the next two months, I want at least one hundred proposals for major or minor improvements from each and every one of you. These proposals are to be based on the results of discussions that you will hold with your subordinates (short rhetorical pause here). To make these discussions easier, we've produced some materials that you can use if you find them helpful.

The latter variant is much more like a dramatic opening, but aside from that, I see these two variants as two different ways of positioning the training. The first variant talks about support for training efforts, while the second indicates a demand for improvements in the company's operations.

This example is also illuminating in that the project was initiated precisely due to a need for improvements in the company's operations—not due to a need for training per se. I've seen many times and in many different situations how a need for change and improvement leads to fairly undemanding (and sometimes free-spending) training programs where there is little connection between the content and form of the training and the problems or needs that the training was originally supposed to solve.

I discussed this matter earlier, but I take it up again because I want to present a few of the questions that should be asked when training needs are being studied.

But first, a few more examples.

On another occasion, I was asked to develop a course in assets management for a large manufacturing company. This was at the end of the seventies, when assets management was in vogue. ("There's gold on the workshop floor," as one industrialist put it.) In discussions with the people involved, who were fairly upper-level managers, I asked them where in the company's operations they saw the greatest potentials. But they had no idea at all.

What do you do in a case like that? The only thing I could reasonably do was to recommend that they first try (with help from a consultant in material administration) to get an idea of where the greatest potentials were, and then try to determine which of these potentials were most worth pursuing—a kind of "doability" analysis. I also suggested that this analysis include at least one good hypothesis as to what behavior on the part of the people involved affected the levels of tied-up capital. Only then could we start talking about training.

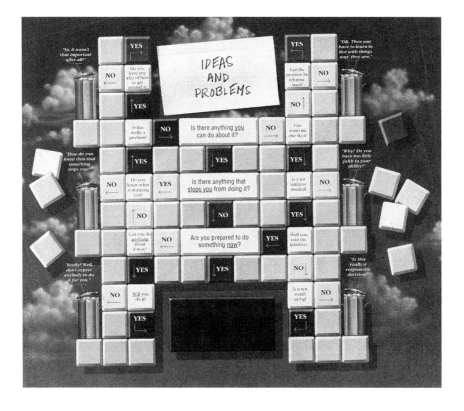

This "idea processor" was one of the learning aids that the food company managers used. Its purpose is to ensure that ideas are brought to conclusion. An idea is placed in the top square. Then the group works through the various questions to determine where the idea winds up: in the waste-paper basket or on a "things-to-do" list.

A similar case at another company: responsibility for capital rationalization was essentially in the hands of the planning and finance departments. The people there didn't have much success in finding the problem, for the simple reason that the high level of tied-up capital wasn't due primarily to problems in the planning system or the financial system.

What they had failed to notice was that the foremen were in the habit of ordering material at least a couple of weeks in advance and stashing it away to make sure they wouldn't run out.

Only when the foremen realized the economic consequences of their behavior did a reduction in their "personal back-up stocks" make any sense to them.

So one of the main conditions for identifying real training needs is to know which people have the greatest influence on whatever is supposed to be changed. It's also necessary to have an idea of what sort of modification in their behavior will probably result in this change.

Only then can we discuss what kind of knowledge (content and quality) is likely to lead to the desired change.

Advice and checklists of this kind can easily become stereotyped hierarchies of the obvious, but they can be helpful if they're related to an existing need.

Therefore, I would ask the reader to pick out a relevant problem area and try to answer the following questions. (I've included these examples to illustrate the thought process involved.)

1. What's the problem, the need? (For example: poor budget follow-up.)
2. Who are the people involved? (For example: mid-level managers, but even the people in charge of the system and of reporting, and, perhaps the management people that wrote the directives.)
3. What kind(s) of behavior must be changed? (For example: late reporting of data, our ways of drawing conclusions from reports, etc.)
4. What external factors control or influence this behavior? (For example: the format of the system and the reports, an inability to see the true value of the budget, etc.)
5. What type of change are we looking for? (This is an important question which, as we can see from the answers to the previous

questions, cannot be answered with sweeping generalizations like "better discipline." Instead, we have to determine what the value of better budget follow-up would be. For example, we can reasonably assume that the value of budget follow-up can best be expressed as "the ability to use our resources in a productive way." We can then focus on this statement and not on budget follow-up per se. So we're suddenly talking about leadership and priorities; budget follow-up is only a tool, not the main subject. Presumably, the need for change then becomes a matter of decision-making and priorities.)

6. What kind of knowledge, insight, or ability is needed to make this change possible? (It can be knowledge of how important the actions of a certain department are for internal and/or external customers. It can include insights into what the company's main strategy and marginal strategy are. It can be knowledge of the characteristics and interests of the company's employees. Or it can simply be a matter of understanding what reports reveal about resource use, and, most of all, what an alternative use of resources would lead to.)

Spending some time and effort on this analysis can save a lot of money. If we're too quick to accept the first thought that comes to mind ("let's hold a two-day course on budget follow-up"), the benefits are likely to be fairly slim.

With an analysis like the one shown above, the probability of drawing the right conclusions increases considerably. The managers in the example will get much more out of their training, because they'll have a chance to learn to take stock of their resources in a constructive way, and to simulate different ways of using them.

They discover for themselves the need for budget follow-up and, possibly, that the present system only partially meets their needs. As a result, the people in charge of the system will also get what they've wanted for a long time: the users' active participation in improving the system further.

Of course, the same sort of reasoning applies very much to you when you participate in a course as a student or when you study independently. A good question to ask yourself at the start is, "What problem could this be a solution to?"

The next question involves behavior. In what activity can the knowledge be of help: in decision-making, setting priorities, customer relations? Then we have to consider what type of change we're looking for. If the main area is, say, "priorities" (our own priorities), the type of change can be "concentrating on the most profitable customers," "better delegation of responsibility," "the ability to determine which factors will be of greatest importance further ahead in the process," etc.

By using your imagination and thinking things through this way, you program yourself to be more receptive to things that can benefit you directly. You'll also get a preliminary idea of whether the course or book is worth spending any time on at all.

The fact that many people don't think they have time for training is a bad sign. If nothing else, it indicates that they've had some bad experiences. As a result (and due to cost increases in general), companies try to cut training time to a minimum.

But the question is how these cuts should be made.

A pedagogical contract

No reader can have failed to recognize my central ideas. First, learners are at least as responsible as the instructor for the way training is carried out. Second, training will give the desired results only if it provides conditions in which the natural learning process can work. To achieve continual increases in training efficiency, the training's "quality control" (evaluation) must include both the instructor's and the students' efforts and acceptance of responsibility, and it has to focus on how well the conditions for learning were fulfilled.

A contract is an agreement on commitments. A pedagogical contract is an agreement on how responsibility for training is to be shared, and this requires that everyone involved have the same understanding of what they have agreed to!

I propose that we replace traditional evaluation forms (How well do you think we have presented the course material?) with a pedagogical contract that helps to define the "rules of the game," and which can serve as the basis for an ongoing evaluation of how well the instructor and the students have succeeded in living up to these commitments. Thus, we get continuous feedback to ensure that resources are being used to the best advantage—that the return obtained is reasonable in relation to the effort expended. I offer an example of such a contract on the following pages.

To get an idea of how a pedagogical contract can be used, try answering the questions on the following pages, using as a model a course, lecture, or speech you've recently attended, or a book you've read.

Then total your points and mark your scores in the graph on page 186 (page 4 of the form). This will give you a graphic representation of your experience and of the return on time spent.

The questions have been grouped into columns and rows. You

can evaluate the extent to which the various conditions for learning were satisfied (the five columns), and the extent to which the course (instructors and material) on the one hand, and the students themselves on the other, contributed to this.

If this agreement is to be worthy of the name "contract," an evaluation at the conclusion isn't enough. Instead, the evaluation criteria for establishing the instructor/learner relationship and the participants' commitments ("signing the contract") should be introduced early in the course, when the course layout is presented (prevaluation). At suitable times during the course, the questions (and the graph on page 4 of the form) can then provide help in determining how successful everyone has been (evaluation).

A pedagogical contract

This form will enable you to perform both a *prevaluation* (beforehand) and an *evaluation* (afterwards) of the quality of a course or course section, and of your own efforts to achieve a high return on time spent.

PREVALUATION

A discussion in advance of how the course will be arranged and of how the participants are to work can

EVALUATION

An evaluation at the end of a course or session will give you a chance to compare the results with your ex-

The questions on the form ask about both the training itself and your own efforts.

PREVALUATION and EVALUATION: A. Answer each of the following questions by choosing an alternative and circling the corresponding number.

1. Was the purpose of the course clear?	2. Was the course content accessible?	3. Did the course awaken your enthusiasm?
a.	**a.**	**a.**
How clear was the purpose (the hoped-for results) of the course? (Circle your answer.)	How suitable were the lectures and course materials in terms of the purpose of the course and the interests of the participants?	How engrossing was the overall experience?
1 Extremely unclear	1 Highly unsuitable	1 No, not nearly enough
2 Fairly unclear	2 Fairly unsuitable	2 Yes, to some extent
3 Fairly clear	3 Fairly suitable	3 Yes, to a fair extent
4 Extremely clear	4 Highly suitable	4 Yes, sufficiently
b.	**b.**	**b.**
To what degree was your participation driven by your perceived need for certain knowledge?	Did you make sure that you were able to keep up with and understand the information given?	How important was it for you to get seriously involved and actively participate?
1 Very little	1 No, I was often lost	1 Not at all important
2 Somewhat	2 Yes, sometimes	2 Slightly important
3 To a fair extent	3 Yes, most of the time	3 Fairly important
4 A lot	4 Yes, all the time	4 Very important
c.	**c.**	**c.**
How well did the purpose of the course coincide with your own needs and interests?	How interesting was the course?	How meaningful to you were the course exercises and discussions?
1 Not at all	1 Fairly uninteresting	1 Fairly meaningless
2 Somewhat	2 Not uninteresting	2 Somewhat meaningful
3 Fairly well	3 Fairly interesting	3 Fairly meaningful
4 Totally	4 Very interesting	4 Very meaningful
☐ Total (a + b + c)	☐ Total (a + b + c)	☐ Total (a + b + c)

THE PEDAGOGICAL CONTRACT: (Note here what you intend to do to ensure good conditions for learning.)

_____ _____ _____

_____ _____ _____

_____ _____ _____

_____ _____ _____

_____ _____ _____

_____ _____ _____

_____ _____ _____

B. Total your scores, first horizontally (to obtain the separate totals for the a, b and c questions) and then vertically. Enter the results on page 4.

4. How much did you learn?	5. Will what you learned be useful to you?	6. TOTALS
a. Was the course arranged in a way that helped you to understand, and to draw your own conclusions? 1 No, not at all 2 Yes, somewhat 3 Yes, a lot 4 Yes, very much so	**a.** Was the course arranged in a manner that helped you find ways to use your new knowledge in practice? 1 No, not at all 2 Yes, somewhat 3 Yes, a lot 4 Yes, very much so	**a.** Add up your scores for the five "a" questions. Circle the corresponding figure (1, 2, 3 or 4). 1 5-10 2 11-14 3 15-17 4 18-20
b. Did you make sure that you got what you wanted in terms of new knowledge? 1 No, not at all 2 Yes, occasionally 3 Yes, most of the time 4 Yes, all the time	**b.** Were you able to create a clear cut vision of how you can use your new knowledge? 1 No, I don't know 2 I have a vague idea 3 Yes, to some extent 4 Yes, I know exactly	**b.** Add up your scores for the five "b" questions. Circle the corresponding figure (1, 2, 3 or 4). 1 5-10 2 11-14 3 15-17 4 18-20
c. Was what you learned important to you? 1 No, not at all 2 Yes, a little 3 Yes, somewhat 4 Yes, very much so	**c.** Do you envision yourself doing things differently as a result of what you've learned? 1 Probably not 2 Perhaps 3 Yes, probably 4 Yes, definitely	**c.** Add up your scores for the five "c" questions. Circle the corresponding figure (1, 2, 3 or 4). 1 5-10 2 11-14 3 15-17 4 18-20
Total (a + b + c)	Total (a + b + c)	Total (a + b + c)

It isn't unreasonable to demand that every course offered within an organization be evaluated this way at the end of the course. If the results are then entered into a data base, changes in the productivity of a company's training program can be monitored continuously.

Mark your scores from the preceding pages on the corresponding six scales in the graph. Draw lines between adjacent points to obtain a graphic image of the strong and weak points of the course and of participant interaction during the course. Interpret the results as follows:

1. **The purpose of the course.** On whose terms was the course presented—on yours or on those of the people running the course? A low score indicates that you were unsure as to the value of participating: "This might be worthwhile," "I'll have to wait and see what they come up with."

2. **The course content.** These questions show the extent to which you felt that the training was a dialogue between you and the instructor. A low score indicates that you were "subjected to training" rather than participated in it: "I didn't get it," "I had trouble concentrating," "I felt like a blockhead," "It was abstract and far too theoretical."

3. **Involvement.** How engrossing was the overall experience? How much control did you have over your own learning process? A low score shows that you had too little opportunity to do any independent thinking: "The pace was too fast, and I couldn't keep up," "It was mostly sausage-stuffing." "I heard what they said but I didn't understand what they meant."

4. **Learning.** How much did you learn? Did you see any reason to get involved? A low score obviously means that the training didn't result in knowledge: "I don't know what, if anything, I learned," "I'll never remember this," "A lot of teaching but not much learning."

5. **Utility.** Will what you learned be useful to you? Has the course increased your expertise or hasn't it? A low score indicates that you had difficulty seeing any connection between the course content and your real-life situation: "Far too theoretical," "I'm going to have to think about this a lot before I can find any use for it," "I'll never have any reason to take the course material off the bookshelf," "The course dealt with a totally different world than the one I live in," "Interesting, but not usable."

6. **Totals.** These totals will give you a rough idea of the return on time spent. A high score reflects an efficient use of resources. If the score was low, you should try to determine whether this was due to the training itself (the "a" questions in the form) or to the quality of your own efforts (the "b" questions). Pay special attention to all low scores (1s and 2s).

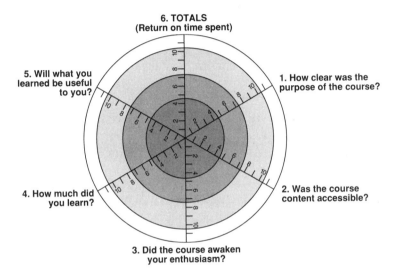

Draw lines between adjacent points to obtain a graphic image of the strong and weak points of the course and of participant interaction during the course. Less than 8 points on a scale can be considered critical. What could/should you have done to improve the outcome? An example is shown below: dashed line = expected outcome (prevaluation); solid line = actual outcome (evaluation).

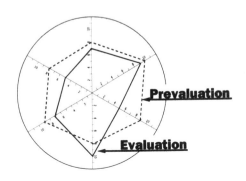

The learning organization

W hy do some companies and organizations, even those manned by discerning, wise, experienced people, appear to be dumb (helpless, incapable of taking action), while others seem to be smart (competent, farsighted)?

One common explanation is that some companies appear to be dumb because its people have different knowledge or conceptions of what the rules are, or different ideas of what has to be done, of what's important, of what the company's goals are.

The term for this is anergy, which means that the whole is less than the sum of its parts. This is the opposite of synergy, where the whole is greater than the sum of its parts (synergy: 2 + 2 = 5; anergy: 2 + 2 = 3).

I use the term "learning organization" to illustrate that there are different ways of organizing and leading a business, and that these different ways foster, to a greater or lesser extent, overall learning, and thus the expertise that constitutes a company's ability to compete.

The terms "learning company" and "learning organization" are far from new, but they have become more relevant as a result of current trends like globalization, stiffer competition, new technologies, fewer employees, more complex (and thus more competition-dependent) products and services, the need to carry out changeovers faster, etc.

As I mentioned earlier, my premise is that traditional ways of organizing and leading a business fail to foster (and even inhibit) learning, and that this is why we need to find new ways of looking at leadership and the distribution of work and responsibility. Some companies have come a long way in this regard, while others are still stuck in the old routines, and still others are involved in the painful process of changing from the old ways to new ones.

So what makes a company a "learning organization"? It's primarily a matter of how well the company succeeds in creating conditions in which all of its people can take joint responsibility for the whole—the business. For example, some learning companies demand that their managers (marketing managers, production managers, development managers, etc.) visit customers frequently, that they assume the roles of competitors' customers, that they work together to find new solutions, that they, together with their subordinates, carry out in-depth analyses of the company's customer base and of what the competitors are doing, and that they invite customers to come in and discuss possible improvements. In the same way, the suppliers of learning companies are also expected to take action. (A typical goal is to reduce the number of primary suppliers radically, and to develop much closer cooperation with those who are left.) A learning company helps its suppliers to develop their expertise and become learning companies themselves: companies that can take responsibility for quality.

In learning companies, a "results chart" is set up near the production line. It includes everything from quality parameters to how the company's sales compare with competitors'.

In addition, learning companies typically employ scouts whose job is to keep abreast of technological advances, to find out whether other companies (and not only competitors) have come up with clever solutions to, say, an administrative problem.

A common characteristic of all learning companies is that they view their people as . . . people.

The results of this work are processed continuously by various development groups, to ensure that any such advances can be used to the company's benefit as soon as possible.

Another characteristic of a learning company is the way it views productivity. As someone said back in 1958 at the conference on productivity in Rome, "Productivity is most of all a state of mind, the desire to continuously improve upon what has already been achieved. . . ." The learning company bases its measurements of productivity solely on simple data directly related to the operation in question.

Thus, the conditions for success can be summarized as follows.

First, everyone must have an overview of the company's activities and goals, and of the direction of future trends. This is popularly called a vision, that is, a living image of what things will be like. It isn't enough for a company to organize its operations so that each individual has responsibility only for his or her little piece of the puzzle. There is a need for a holistic view, where each individual knows what role he or she is playing in the company's overall operations.

Just as we used a jigsaw puzzle broken up into pieces as an analogy for traditional forms of organization, we can use the hologram as an analogy for the new one. Laser beams are used to create a hologram, and the result is a three-dimensional "photograph" with the correct depth. If we break a hologram plate into pieces, each piece—unlike a puzzle piece—will show the entire picture, but the perspective will be different and the picture will be smaller.

Second, each individual must have continuous access to information (data) on all advances that are important for the company's success. It isn't enough to implement traditional information systems that are limited to historical, financial data. It's just as important to know the answer to a question like "How satisfied are our customers with our quality?" as it is to one like "Has department X gone over budget?"

Third, people in the company must have a chance to learn from each other and to draw joint conclusions about what needs to be done. It isn't enough for the boss alone to know what's going on, and to decide how resources (time, money, expertise) should be used.

The Worker's Plea:
1. **Don't stifle my natural curiosity; awaken it!**
   In other words, don't take the "compass" away from me. Give me some independence; let me take part from the beginning, and create my own idea of why I should get involved.

2. **Just give me the information I need, not a lot of**

information I don't need.
In other words, I respect your knowledge, and I thank you for wanting to share it with me, but remember that the only reason you've been appointed to be my supervisor is to give me the information that I need—the information that's meaningful to me.

3. **Let me think things through myself and draw my own conclusions.**
In other words, don't abandon me, don't deny me my own path to conclusions and insight. Hold your enthusiasm and your impatience in check. Don't believe that your own conclusions, based on your many years of experience, can be mine just because you tell me what they are.

4. **Help me find contexts for the things I've understood!**
In other words, when you see that I understand, that I'm feeling it in my bones and saying "Aha!," help me find words and expressions for the things I've understood, so I can turn my insights into knowledge that I can handle.

5. **Help me use my knowledge, so it doesn't wither away and become useless.**
In other words, give me a chance to test and expand and reinforce my knowledge. Show me how I can use it, so I can continue to learn on my own, aided by new experiences.

A new management style is emerging (again!). Here's a short version of management history. First, the boss was a boss who ran the company by issuing instructions (MBI, management by instructions). Then the boss was a leader who controlled the operation by setting goals (MBO, management by objectives). Later the boss was also supposed to be a coach who stimulated, involved, and motivated his people (MBWA, management by walking around).

Today, moreover, the boss is expected to train, and learn together with, his or her subordinates (MBL, management by learning), and thus, to share leadership responsibilities with them.

Of course, one common characteristic of all learning organizations is that they view their people as . . . people.

Another is that they look at their business as an integrated system, and not as a linear chain of events. The linear view is based on the idea that management can run a company by making plans and issuing instructions, as in a central-planning economy, while leaders with a systematic perspective try to create conditions for "self-organization," as in a free-market economy—obviously within established parameters or standards related to time, quality, etc. To ensure adherence to these standards, internal systems must be implemented which require that all activities be followed by feedback of one kind or another within an extremely short time, perhaps as little as a few days.

Not surprisingly, the conditions for learning seem to be generally the same for companies (and for groups and teams) as they are for individuals:

- access to a meaningful overall view (vision);
- access to relevant information;
- opportunities to process the information, in order to gain individual (joint) insights, conclusions and understanding;
- a common view of what the consequences of these conclusions and this understanding will be for the company as a whole;
- plans (and resources) for turning words into action.

Thus, "the student's plea" is "the worker's plea," just as the principles for teaching and learning are the principles for leadership.

At least for people and companies who have understood what management in the 90s will be like.

And that's the whole idea.

Index

A MANAGER'S GUIDE TO GLOBALIZATION
Six Keys to Success in a Changing World
Stephen H Rhinesmith
Co-published by the American Society for Training and Development/Irwin Professional Publishing
Discover the six key skills needed to effectively compete in an increasingly internationally-challenging environment. Rhinesmith shows you how to: Develop a corporate culture that allows your organization to adapt to a world of constant change.
ISBN: 1-55623-904-1

THE CORPORATE TRAINER'S QUICK REFERENCE
Geoffrey Moss
Concisely covers the basics of training to help organizations eliminate wasted time and ensure that the process runs smoothly. Geoffrey Moss includes dozens of checklists, charts, and tips that show readers how to effectively analyze the trainees to target the information in the training session.
ISBN: 1-55623-905-x

GLOBAL TRAINING
How to Design a Program for the Multinational Corporation
Sylvia B. Odenwald
Co-published by the American Society for Training and Development/ Business One Irwin
Shows companies how to research, develop, and implement an international training program. Organized to create and adapt custom training courses, this resource offers how-to tips that make application of the ideas presented as easy as possible.
ISBN: 1-55623-986-6

THE LIVING ORGANIZATION
Transforming Teams into Workplace Communities
John Nirenberg
Co-published by Pfeiffer & Company/Irwin Professional Publishing
Shows managers the next step after teams—creating a workplace community. This guide lays out a blueprint for this type of transformation with real-world examples and a how-to strategy for turning around a disenchanted work force.
ISBN: 1-55623-943-2

EVALUATING TRAINER EFFECTIVENESS
Leslie Rae
Provides a method that results in useful information for the organization, client, and trainer through effective assessment of the trainer and training program. Along with tips for evaluation by the trainees, this reference includes forms, checklists, and guidelines that go beyond the standard "How would you rate this session overall?"
ISBN: 1-55623-881-9

Available at fine bookstores and libraries everywhere.